Saving Beauty

Luther,   "God writes the Gospel, not in the Bible alone,
but on trees and clouds and flowers and
stars."

creation = an accessible mirror of
the Beauty of an infinite God.

Plato "Beautiful things are difficult"

Define the relationship between
World Created w/ Natural Beauty
and Human Creatures made to Experience the beauty

Saving Beauty

A Theological Aesthetics of Nature

Kathryn B. Alexander

Fortress Press
Minneapolis

SAVING BEAUTY
A Theological Aesthetics of Nature

Copyright © 2014 Fortress Press. All rights reserved. Except for brief quotations
in critical articles or reviews, no part of this book may be reproduced in any
manner without prior written permission from the publisher. Visit
http://www.augsburgfortress.org/copyrights/ or write to Permissions, Augsburg
Fortress, Box 1209, Minneapolis, MN 55440.

Cover image: The big tree Rickychau78/iStock/Thinkstock
Cover design: Tory Herman

Library of Congress Cataloging-in-Publication Data
Print ISBN: 978-1-4514-7223-3
eBook ISBN: 978-1-4514-8756-5

The paper used in this publication meets the minimum requirements of
American National Standard for Information Sciences — Permanence of Paper
for Printed Library Materials, ANSI Z329.48-1984.

Manufactured in the U.S.A.

This book was produced using PressBooks.com, and PDF rendering was done by
PrinceXML.

In loving memory of my mother Claire Bellm
my encourager of Beauty

In loving memory of Alejandro García-Rivera
my teacher of Beauty

In thanksgiving for Margaret Miles, Jay Johnson,
Rosemary Ruether & Frank Oppenheim
my shepherds through Beauty

In thanksgiving for my husband Jason Alexander
my companion in Beauty

And offered for my children: Luke, Nate & Anna
may their lives be filled with Beauty

Contents

Introduction

In "Field Notes for an Aesthetic of Storms," Kathleen Moore ponders the reason why she has chased after storms since childhood, finding them irresistible even as they are frightening. She describes, for example, playing in a lightning storm as a child with her sisters, reaching out their hands toward rocks and watching the rocks buzz more intensely, the closer the girls came. "We skipped and spun mindlessly in the electric charges, creating music with our bodies, the way children dance in fountains and make music with splashing light. Certainly this was stupid, but it was also irresistible."[1] As an adult Moore finds herself still searching out the wildness of storms, flirting with the edge of them, and wondering why. She considers and then dismisses several possible reasons, from whether the excitement of a storm might be some kind of physiological or cellular "high" to whether the joy of a storm is to be found in the fact that one survived or even that one has been purged in some way of strong emotion, as Aristotle would describe the experience of watching a Greek tragedy. Finally she arrives at the idea that, despite their destructiveness, storms might attract because there is <u>something *beautiful*</u> about them.

1. Kathleen Dean Moore, "Field Notes for an Aesthetic of Storms," 53–63 in her *Holdfast: At Home in the Natural World* (New York: Lyons Press, 1999), 55.

To examine this theory Moore invokes the memory of a particularly harsh storm experienced during a camping trip. She found the storm beautiful, even though there were terrifying moments. In the midst of it she experienced a heightened excitement, a close focus, an intensity close to fear. This was, she believed, an experience of sublimity: "the blow-to-the-gut awareness of chaotic forces unleashed and uncontrolled, the terror—and finally the awe. To experience the sublime is to understand, with an insight so fierce and sudden it makes you duck, that there is power and possibility in the universe greater than anyone can imagine. The sublime blows out the boundaries of human experience. Is this, finally, what we crave?"[2]

I am intrigued by Moore's question. I, too, have suspected that the experience of awe in the natural world is something we crave, precisely as the experience "blows out the boundaries" and we find ourselves suddenly engaged in a radically expanded or comprehensive insight of some kind. What is the nature of this insight? How does the beauty of creation, much less an experience of the "sublime," lead to such an insight? And, perhaps most importantly, how are we changed as a result of this kind of encounter with the beautiful? In chasing after storms, Moore has touched on a profoundly theological set of questions.

In light of the devastating complexity of the environmental crisis, to speak of experiencing natural beauty seems a very small thing. As a touch point for theological reflection, beauty at its strongest seems fragile, fleeting, and potentially to be found only a single step above romanticism or sentimentalism. At worst it may seem distracting or elitist to speak of natural beauty, or perhaps even an escapist turning from the difficult work at hand, of creating economic and political changes that are key to more ecologically sound living

2. Ibid., 62.

across the globe. Despite these challenges, if Fyodor Dostoevsky was right that beauty will save the world,[3] then speaking of beauty, particularly beauty in the natural world, is now a necessity. Further, an examination of the experience of natural beauty has the potential to illumine the environmental crisis as a spiritual crisis.

If Moore is correct that we crave experiences of awe and sublimity in nature, why are we destroying what we fundamentally crave? We seem to be shattering the very context that makes us fully human in a created order that, by divine design, includes beauty. This is the nature of the spiritual crisis: how can our craving for natural beauty be reconciled with human destruction of the natural world? This spiritual crisis is one born of the short-sightedness of human appetites for consumption and unsustainable patterns of living, and one of disconnectedness from beauty.

Solving environmental threats and disasters, and now global climate change, is what Thomas Berry has called the Great Work facing humankind. Never before in our history have we faced such a complex challenge, the solution to which requires engagement by every kind of human ingenuity and creativity. One small piece of this great work is answering the spiritual crisis named above. Such an answer can come from natural beauty as a source of religious insight.

American philosopher Josiah Royce suggested that religious insights shed light on the knowledge of the need and way of salvation. He believed that "salvation" is guidance toward understanding and accomplishing the highest aims of human life, which we are ever in danger of missing. That guidance, Royce suggested, must come from outside ourselves, from a source of insight. Beauty, he claimed, is one such source, though he remained largely silent on the subject. This project explores natural beauty as a

3. A phrase widely quoted from *The Idiot*, first published in English in 1887.

3

Natural Beauty as source of religious insight

source of religious insight, an insight that is critical to answering the spiritual crisis we face.

The consideration of natural beauty is now a theological imperative in two senses: how does beauty save, and how do we save beauty? What is the connection between ecological salvation (saving beauty) and human salvation (beauty saving)? My aim in this project is not to attempt an exhaustive statement about the nature of human salvation or Christology in light of the environmental crisis but to consider the relationship between the experience of natural beauty and insight into the need for human salvation. What does beauty have to say to our souls, particularly at a time when it seems that the beauty of creation is slipping away with ever-increasing environmental degradation? What insight can we achieve in those experiences that might help us to deepen our understanding of the highest aims and goals of human life? And further, how might the story of our salvation be linked to the salvation of beauty that is all around us?

In this book I will examine the experience of natural beauty as a source of religious insight and develop a theological aesthetics of nature. The project's motivation is my conviction that a necessary ingredient of ecological redemption is the role that natural beauty can play in illuminating the need and way of human salvation. Three areas of inquiry will constitute the foundation of this work. The first is a historical overview of theological aesthetics with particular attention to the relationship between natural beauty and soteriology in the writings of representative figures in the history of Christian thought. Second, I will draw upon the philosophy of American pragmatist Josiah Royce (1855–1916), exploring his understanding of the nature of religious insight into the way and need of salvation, as well as his view of the ways in which beauty and art are sources of such insight. The third aspect of this work is an engagement with the works of British environmental artist Andy Goldsworthy (b. 1956), whose art reveals natural beauty in such profoundly different ways that with theological reflection we are able to experience natural beauty as a source of religious insight. He uses found objects in nature to blur the boundaries between human aesthetics and natural beauty, thus raising critical philosophical questions about the nature of beauty and the nature of "nature" in relationship to humanity. His art suggests a connection between human art and natural beauty, rejecting a dualism between culture and landscape. This connection is a source of religious insight in the Roycean sense, one that opens up the possibility of a theological aesthetics of nature. Such an insight reveals an integral view of redemption that includes both the human and the natural world.

In chapter one, I will undertake a brief theological history of natural beauty, exploring the various roles it has inhabited in understandings of human redemption. For centuries before the scientific revolution, theologians spoke of God in a world that was alive, organically filled with the Good, the True, and the Beautiful. Beauty as natural revelation or reflection of God was at their fingertips. With the rise of modern science and economics and a radically readjusted worldview and theology, theologians began to speak less of beauty in the now mechanistic universe. Further, sixteenth-century Christian reform movements planted seeds of a fiercely tenacious iconoclasm, the fruits of which remain with us in the struggle to determine a right relationship with nature (now depraved) and in a tragic suspicion about whether beauty has anything to teach. Since the Enlightenment the perception of beauty, or the experience of the beautiful, has been relegated to the subjective realm and to matters of taste. Speaking of beauty today in the development of a theological aesthetics is thus a great challenge. Yet, despite modern obstacles, a trajectory can be found throughout the history of Christian thought in which the experience of natural beauty has been understood as significant to human redemption, and this is what I trace in the first chapter.

In describing the work of the second chapter I should first say that the term "theological aesthetics" has proven difficult to define. I draw upon the definition offered by Alejandro García-Rivera, who took Alexander Baumgarten's eighteenth-century definition of aesthetics as the philosophy and science of the beautiful, or the science of sensory cognition, and recast it into theological terms, looking at the science of what moves the human heart. This "brings us closer to the mysterious experience of the truly beautiful . . . an experience that holds the most persuasive claim to being what has become an *aporia* in our day, the real universal . . . . Theological aesthetics recognizes in the experience of the truly beautiful a religious dimension." [4] In casting aesthetics in this light and drawing on the pre-modern tradition of transcendentals, García-Rivera opened the door of aesthetic theory to a profound question about the experience of the beautiful.

A theological aesthetics seeks to affirm the human capacity to know and love God as Beauty through experiences of the beautiful. Further, a theological aesthetics suggests that there is a religious aspect to the experience of the beautiful that is revelatory and redemptive. As Hans Urs von Balthasar suggests, we know God through our senses. Thus the experience of earthly beauty can deepen our knowledge of the divine. A premise of theological aesthetics is that the experience of the beautiful is redemptive; the task is to explore how. For this I turn in chapter two to the interpretive theory of Josiah Royce.

Sensory Cognition

what moves to human heart.

Know & Love God thru the Beautiful

Know God thru Senses

To Exp Beauty is Redemptive

4. From Alejandro García-Rivera, *The Community of the Beautiful: A Theological Aesthetics* (Collegeville, MN: Liturgical Press, 1999), 9.

Though he did not have an explicit theory of aesthetics, Royce developed a philosophy of religious insight that is central to this project. In *Sources of Religious Insight* he begins with insight in general, defining it as "knowledge that makes us aware of the unity of many facts in one whole, and that at the same time brings us into intimate personal contact with these facts and with the whole wherein they are united."[5] There are three marks of an insight: breadth of range, coherence and unity of view, and closeness of personal touch. Further, according to Royce, an insight is religious when its object is religious, and a religious insight is essentially redemptive. In short, religious insight is knowledge of the need and way of salvation.

¬ sources of religious insight

Royce offered seven sources of religious insight, including personal experience, social experience, reason, will, dedicated loyalty, the religious mission of sorrow, and finally the Unity of the Spirit and the Invisible Church. Taken together and integrated, they represent a process of illumination open to all, beginning with individual experience and culminating in corporate experience. Though he hesitated to speak formally of beauty, he understood clearly that art and natural beauty are also sources that can yield insight into the need and way of salvation and ultimately draw one who experiences beauty redemptively into community. One aim of this project is to develop Royce's idea that natural beauty is a source of religious insight.

Is Natural Beauty a source of Religious insight

Chapter three is an exploration of the art of Andy Goldsworthy, whose work with found objects in nature reveals nature itself to us in ways we would not otherwise notice. His creations brilliantly blur the boundaries between human works of art and natural beauty, raising critical philosophical questions about the nature of beauty and

5. Josiah Royce, *Sources of Religious Insight* (Washington, DC: Catholic University of America Press, 2001), 5–6.

7

the nature of "nature" in relationship to humanity. His works also illustrate the themes of time and decay or transience, a fascinating tension between human and divine creation, and the cyclical notion of creation and destruction, all of which are fruitful themes for ecological theology. I consider the origins and landscapes of land art, form, and process used in Goldsworthy's work, on which critiques are deeply divided, and finally propose a reconceptualization: that nature and culture are not dualistic but both contained in the idea of "landscape." I explore these issues to illumine my broader aim, which is to demonstrate a continuum between aesthetics and natural beauty. This connection is a source of religious insight in the Roycean sense, one that opens up the possibility of a theological aesthetics of nature, which is developed as the central theme in chapter four. Such an insight reveals an integral view of redemption that includes both the human and the natural world, a view critically needed for our time.

My intent in this work is to suggest that we can no longer consider soteriological questions in isolation from our environment and to show that there is a connection between beauty in creation and insight into the human need for salvation. I hope to provide understanding about this connection and to demonstrate theologically the ways in which we need beauty. I hope that this work also addresses what moves us to respond to ecological devastation. As suggested above, with many others I believe that the environmental crisis is, at heart, a spiritual crisis[6] and that this is one aspect among many that needs to be addressed within and by

6. In "An Open Letter to the Religious Community," scientists (many of whom are avowed atheists) appealed to the world religious community to engage the environmental crisis. "Problems of such magnitude, and solutions demanding so broad a perspective, must be recognized as having a religious as well as a scientific dimension. Mindful of our common responsibility, we scientists, many of us long engaged in combating the environmental crisis, urgently appeal to the world religious community to commit, in word and deed, and as boldly as is required, to preserve the environment of the Earth. . . . As scientists, many of us have had profound experiences of awe and reverence before the universe. We understand that what is regarded as sacred is more likely to be treated with care and respect. . . ." (Carl Sagan, et al., "An

religious communities. I believe there is a place and a need for beauty in the conversation.

In the conclusion I will explore the role of beauty in what "geologian" Thomas Berry often calls our ecological age. He suggests that beauty holds a key to what moves us to address the issues at hand:

Destroy Living forms = destroy Modes of divine presence

> We should be clear about what happens when we destroy the living forms of this planet. The first consequence is that we destroy modes of divine presence. If we have a wonderful sense of the divine, it is because we live amid such awesome magnificence. If we have refinement of emotion and sensitivity, it is because of the delicacy, the fragrance, and the indescribable beauty of song and music and rhythmic movement in the world about us . . . . If we lived on the moon, our mind and emotions, our speech, our imagination, our sense of the divine would all reflect the desolation of the lunar landscape.[7]

Beauty has something to do with our understandings of the divine, of ourselves, and of the relationship of both to the natural world. And there is growing intuition that beauty has something to do with human redemption and our ability to see those divine modes of presence and achieve that "wonderful sense of the divine." Such intuition, or insight, hints that the experience of the beautiful in creation has something to say to our souls, and the message is of great importance not only for our knowledge of God but also for how we ought to live. In short, we crave beauty, we destroy beauty, and we can achieve religious insight from beauty before it is too late. The contribution of beauty to ecological theology, I believe, needs to be fully explored.

Open Letter to the Religious Community," January 1990. Available at http://earthrenewal.org/Open_letter_to_the_religious_.htm.
7. Thomas Berry, *The Dream of the Earth* (San Francisco: Sierra Club Books, 1988), 11.

1

Natural Beauty

A Theological History

There is a sacred place in central <u>Arkansas</u> that is known only to locals, who refer to it simply as "the camp." They are speaking of <u>Camp Mitchell</u>, a retreat center owned and operated by the Episcopal Diocese of Arkansas. The camp is perched on the edge of a dramatic bluff on top of <u>Petit Jean Mountain</u>, the only high place for miles. Cabins look out over a lush valley made up of a patchwork of farmland and wilderness. Birds soar high over the meeting houses, taking prayers and human imagination with them. There is a sense of stillness there, a place where time slows and busyness subsides. And in the middle of the camp lies a small, unassuming chapel that is easy to miss at first glance. From the front, the building looks like just another cabin. The surprise comes when one enters and discovers that there are no walls on the sides and very few items that would suggest a consecrated place. There are as few artificial boundaries as possible between the worshiper and the natural place. Rustic folding chairs face forward, and one's eyes are drawn to the altar, a bare table with a floor-to-ceiling open view behind it of the beautiful valley. Above the altar hangs a simple wooden cross, suspended by thin wire, a form that takes its place in the patchwork landscape below. The cross in the landscape invites those who have come to the camp to experience their faith in the context of natural beauty, and it provides a powerful image for the relationship between the drama of human salvation and natural beauty.

Martin Luther once said, "God writes the gospel not in the Bible alone, but on trees and flowers and clouds and stars."[1] For centuries, theologians have explored the beauty of creation as an agent within human salvation. Various roles have been ascribed to that beauty over time, from that of consolation for pilgrims while on earth or of a finite, accessible mirror of God's own infinite beauty to a means of conversion to Christ. What follows is an attempt to trace the history of theological reflection on the beauty of nature in relation to matters of soteriology. Beginning with the early church, and moving through the medieval church, sixteenth-century reform movements, and the Enlightenment and nineteenth century, I discuss eras within that history broadly, offering a closer look at representative theologians in each. As this history cannot be understood apart from the history of aesthetics, I also explore relevant trends and shifts in philosophical aesthetics as they influence theological developments.

The Early Church: Achieving a Vision of Beauty

A theological history of natural beauty must begin not with early church writers but with Western classical understandings of beauty and art, for these played a significant role in the shaping of Christian

---

1. Martin Luther, *Watchwords for the Warfare of Life,* trans. Elizabeth Rundle Charles (New York: M. W. Dodd, 1869), 191.

thought on beauty. Plato (ca. 424–347 B.C.E.) once wrote: χαλεπὰ τὰ καλά, "beautiful things are difficult."[2] With this proverb he set the stage for the struggle to understand the nature of beauty and its relationship to the divine and to humanity that has challenged theologians for centuries. Describing beauty has proven to be an art in itself, as pinning down the nature of beauty through language has been highly elusive, or in Plato's word, difficult.

An exploration of classical understandings of both art and beauty shows quickly that modern notions of beauty and fine arts were unknown in the classical world. Art was understood as craft. What was beautiful was that which was a perfection of craft. Beauty in the ancient world, either in art or in natural beauty, consisted in correct proportions and arrangement of parts. Harmony and symmetry were essential. Mathematical expressions in particular were considered ideal for conveying this. In "The Great Theory of Beauty and Its Decline," Polish philosopher Wladyslaw Tatarkiewicz defines the classical theory of beauty, based largely on Hellenistic concepts, as comprised of the following aspects:

- Beauty consists in the proportions of the parts.
- The beautiful object is one that displays a consonance of distinct parts.
- The beautiful object has a certain brightness or brilliance about it.
- The beautiful object has integrity or perfection.
- The beautiful object yields pleasure upon contemplation.[3]

Each of these aspects of the "great theory" plays a significant role in early Christian writings on beauty.

2. Plato, *Greater Hippias*, LCL, Plato IV (Cambridge, MA: Harvard University Press, 1977), 304.
3. Wladyslaw Tatarkiewicz, *A History of Ideas: An Essay in Aesthetics* (Warsaw: Polish Scientific Publishers, 1980), chap. 4.

[handwritten annotation: Beautiful = Καλου opposite shameful - dishonest]

It is important to examine the ancient Greek word for "beautiful" as we explore classical conceptions of art and beauty. The Greek word καλός is significantly broader in definition than the modern English "beautiful" and refers to good, right, proper, fitting, better, honorable, honest, fine, beautiful, and/or precious qualities. In English we say that the opposite of beautiful is ugly, but in Greek it is αίσχρός (disgraceful, shameful, dishonest).[4]

Turning to the founder of philosophical aesthetics, with Plato we discover Beauty in the realm of ideal forms and contrasted with imperfect, sensuous beauty. According to Plato, art, understood as *technē*, belonged properly to the realm of forms, not ideas, and assumed a knowing and a making: knowing the end to be achieved and the best means for arriving that end. Art was excellent if the piece demonstrated proportion and measure, which in turn involved the good and the beautiful. Art, or *technē*, was imitative in nature and served the interests of the *polis*. This was true of all the arts except poetry, of which Plato was suspicious. Poets ran the risk of transgressing imitative art. As philosopher Albert Hofstadter writes of Plato's poet,

> The poet is inspired, a winged, holy thing, filled with the power of the divine, hence mad in a noble way far above ordinary knowledge and consciousness. It is this possession that enables him to achieve the authentically artistic that is more than *technē*. Conscious, rational intellect cannot reduce this to a rule, nor can the man who commands *technē* raise himself to the genuinely poetic without divine assistance.[5]

Poets, as the exception to the rule for artists, had the potential to disrupt the social order because of their unruled creativity that

---

4. Barbara Aland, et al., *The Greek New Testament, Fourth Revised Edition* (Stuttgart: Deutsche Bibelgesellschaft, 2001), 91.
5. Albert Hofstadter, *Philosophies of Art and Beauty: Selected Readings in Aesthetics from Plato to Heidegger* (Chicago: University of Chicago Press, 1964), 5.

surpasses the imitative function of *technē*. The ancient artist was supposed to uncover, not invent. Together, the artist with *technē* and the poet with unruled creativity and access to the "authentically artistic," as well as the individual in pursuit of erotic love, as in *The Symposium*, represent Plato's concept of achieving the vision of beauty, each to one's own capacity. There is a beauty in the ideal realm that is inaccessible, yet is approachable through sensuous art and beauty. This idea would play a significant role in the aesthetics of Augustine of Hippo as well as other early Christian writers.

Aristotle (384–322 B.C.E.) expanded Plato's concept of beauty by adding the idea of pleasure. For Aristotle, art had an efficient cause; it was not spontaneous creativity but began with a concept. Art fell within the virtue of making, in the practical intellect, and combined form and matter. Art was fundamentally intellectual, as by it an idea is impressed upon matter. One of Aristotle's key innovations was the idea that art, being good, is also pleasant. Thomas Aquinas (1225–1274) picked up on this thread in his own understanding that "beautiful things are those which please when seen. Hence beauty consists in due proportion; for the senses delight in things duly proportioned . . ."[6] Thomas goes on to define "duly proportioned" as including "three conditions: integrity or perfection, since those things which are impaired are by the very fact ugly; due proportion or harmony; and lastly brightness, or clarity (*claritas*), whence things are called beautiful which have bright color."[7] Drawing thus on Aristotle, Thomas adds the *experience* of the beautiful to his definition, opening the theological door for the idea that the practical realm of the beautiful (i.e., that which can be experienced) participates in some manner in the transcendental realm. For earthly beauty,

Experience Beauty = Transcendental

6. Thomas Aquinas, *Summa Theologiae*, Blackfriars ed. (New York: McGraw-Hill, 1964), I, Q. 5, art. 4.
7. Ibid., I, Q. 39, art. 8.

Thomas Aquinas

this idea implies throughout Christian aesthetics—until the modern period—that natural beauty participates in some manner in divine beauty, and that what we can experience here on earth brings us closer to God.

Neoplatonist philosopher Plotinus (ca. 205–270 C.E.) upheld the distinction between the perfect beauty of ideas and imperfect, sensuous beauty, and added (to the ancient theory of beauty thus far) the soul, which illuminates the proportions. With Plotinus we have moved to the realm of splendor. For him, religion and aesthetics were inextricably linked; like the Hellenistic philosophers before him, he was more concerned with the recognition or vision of beauty, a primary characteristic of reality, at the level of perception rather than with art and human creativity per se.[8] Beauty in the realm of ideas was the archetype for sensual beauty, and glimpses could be seen in the brilliance, including that of natural beauty, emanating from the divine One. In *On the Divine Names,* Pseudo-Dionysius (d. early 6th century) develops Plotinus's primary concern for divine splendor as he writes about beauty as consisting in proportion and brilliance, as seen (i.e., experienced in the sensory order) in divine emanation.[9] Thus from Plato to the early Christian writers we can see a progression in the idea of beauty from a virtually inaccessible existence in the ideal realm to a beauty that emanates in unity from the divine realm and shines within created beauty. In each step of this progression there remains the fundamental problem of how to achieve a vision of that higher or divine beauty and the question of the relationship between the achievement of that vision and human salvation or fulfillment.

8. Margaret R. Miles, *Plotinus on Body and Beauty: Society, Philosophy, and Religion in Third-century Rome* (Oxford: Blackwell, 1999), chap. 2.

9. Tartarkiewicz, *History of Ideas,* 127.

Notes on Early Christian Art

It is against this backdrop of classical understandings of beauty that Christian art emerged. There is a commonly held yet erroneous interpretation of early Christianity as imageless and aniconic before the fourth century. The assumption is often made that the early church had an aversion to images from its Jewish roots, which was then overcome with Constantine's conversion. This argument is far to simplistic. In an iconographic study of the Ancient Near East, Othmar Keel has demonstrated that Judaism was rich in visual arts as a means of expressing an experience of God, though not to depict God directly. The command against images, he argues, was about representing the presence of God, not the ability to represent God by a copy understood as only a copy. Take, for example, the cherubim on the Ark of the Covenant. They signal God's presence. The images themselves are not the presence.[10]

A second, related argument is often made that early Christians resisted the use of images as a practice they associated with pagan culture, thus rejecting the classical aesthetics described thus far. However, as we will see below, several prevalent images from the surrounding cultures made their way into the early art of catacombs and house churches.[11] These two aniconic arguments were widely held through the mid-twentieth century. Eminent art historians at the time portrayed the earliest Christians as proto-Protestants: puritanical, anti-worldly, and opposed to images in worship and to visual art in general.[12] Yet early extant works offer a more nuanced view of the emergence of a distinctly Christian use of images.

10. See Othmar Keel, *The Symbolism of the Biblical World: Ancient Near Eastern Iconography and the Book of Psalms*, trans. Timothy J. Hallett (Winona Lake: Eisenbrauns, 1997).
11. Robin Margaret Jensen, *Understanding Early Christian Art* (New York: Routledge, 2000), 13.
12. Ibid., 14.

The most popular images from a primary source of early Christian art, the catacombs of Rome and its environs, include a wide range of themes, both secular and sacred: banquets, Christ as a shepherd carrying a sheep, Christ as a philosopher teaching his disciples, scenes from the Hebrew Bible and less frequently scenes from the New Testament, and most commonly a repertoire of images found on Jewish, secular, and Christian tombs. These last include flowers and foliage, Roman gods, and *orantes*, figures common in classical painting, with arms lifted in prayer.[13]

There are two significant themes that are missing from the extant images prior to the fourth century. There were no naturalistic portraits of Christ, and there was no depiction of the crucifixion until 432. Constantine outlawed crucifixion in the early fourth century, but it took several years for the associations of a dishonorable death to fade and the crucifix to be understood as a triumphant image. As evidenced in house churches and catacombs alike, Christians seemed to prefer themes of life and deliverance, even in times of persecution. They tended to choose images of peace, not death.[14]

Once portraits of Christ emerged, they varied greatly in form and style. Perhaps this can be attributed to the inculturation of the Christian message, in which just as no single gospel or text could convey the varied experiences of Christ in diverse communities, the same was true of a single image of Christ. With the development of icons a more complex relationship between community and image would emerge, in which an image could convey both likeness and presence.[15]

13. Ibid., 58–61.
14. Margaret R. Miles, *The Word Made Flesh: A History of Christian Thought* (Malden, MA: Blackwell, 2005), 61.
15. See Hans Belting, *Likeness and Presence: A History of the Image before the Era of Art*, trans. Edmund Jephcott (Chicago: University of Chicago Press, 1994).

In her masterful exploration of early Christian art, Robin Jensen argues that, in early Christian communities, texts and images must be interpreted together. Visual and literary images balance and reinforce each other. Texts alone only give a partial view of the experiences of the earliest communities, which must not be oversimplified as aniconic. Profoundly incarnational visual images "provide an extraordinary testimony to the hopes, values, and deeply held convictions of the early Christian communities."[16]

Augustine of Hippo

Having explored briefly some classical understandings of art and beauty and their general influence on the development of early Christian aesthetics, as well as the beginnings of a primitive Christian visual art under both hostile and emergent conditions, we now turn to Augustine of Hippo (354–430) as a representative voice of the early church on the subject of natural beauty. His efforts to understand the role of natural beauty in relationship to soteriology might be best described as an attempt, with Platonic overtones, to achieve a vision of beauty, which is also attaining a vision of God and thus the fulfillment of human life. For Augustine, at the heart of theological aesthetics lies the problem of theodicy, and earthly beauty speaks in particular redemptive ways to pilgrims (post-Fall) on earth. What follows is a threefold exploration of Augustine's aesthetics: (1) a consideration of his wrestling with the problem of evil in the *Confessions* and his use of physical vision as a model for describing the fulfillment of human life, (2) a look at his aesthetic theory of numbers in relation to vision, and (3) an exploration of the role natural or earthly beauty plays in his vision of resurrected life in *The*

16. Jensen, *Understanding Early Christian Art*, 31.

City of God, both as consolation for pilgrims while on earth and as a vestige of God's greater blessings to come. It becomes clear that, for Augustine, achieving a vision of beauty was nothing short of a matter of salvation.

The Problem of Evil

At the heart of Augustine's aesthetics is the question of theodicy. This is perhaps best seen in the story of his conversion to Christianity in the autobiographical *Confessions*, in which he provides a sustained account of his struggle with his own will burdened by sin and oriented away from God. One of the greatest challenges to a reader today in exploring Augustine's answer to the mystery of evil in the *Confessions*[17] is that for Augustine the problem lies not in a seeming contradiction in God's nature, as seen, for example, in David Hume's modern conception of the problem of evil, which is rooted in an Enlightenment optimism about human reason,[18] but rather in the individual human will. Reacting against his previously held Manichaean understanding of evil as a material force in the universe, Augustine opts for a more Platonic conception of evil as a perversion of the will.

Augustine's description of evil in Book VII comes immediately before the recounting of his conversion; his language about evil must be understood in the context of his desire to be released from the chains of the compulsive chasing of desires, or concupiscence. G. R.

---

17. Based on the translation by R. S. Pine-Coffin, *The Confessions of Saint Augustine* (Harmondsworth: Penguin, 1961).
18. Millard J. Erickson, "The Problem of Evil," in *The Blackwell Encyclopedia of Modern Christian Thought,* ed. Alister E. McGrath (Oxford: Blackwell, 1993), 192. Hume offers the following succinct formulation of the problem (or mystery) of evil: either God is willing to prevent evil but not able, or God is able but not willing. In the first case God is not omnipotent. In the second case God is malevolent. If God is neither malevolent nor compromised in potency, how then do we explain evil?

Evans suggests that everything Augustine says about evil must be read in light of a single idea, that "the effect of evil upon the mind is to make it impossible for the sinner to think clearly, and especially to understand higher, spiritual truths and abstract ideas."[19] Thus evil impedes one's ability to see divine beauty. Prior to his conversion Augustine writes of having difficulty with solving the problem of evil when posed as a metaphysical question of the relationship between matter and evil, and of how God might infuse the world in a corporeal sense. Evans argues that it becomes clear to Augustine that he has been using the wrong faculty of perception to try to solve the challenge of the Manichaeans.[20] With this realization he begins to move in more of a Platonic direction, focusing on the problem of evil as a question of the proper orientation of his will toward God. Concupiscence might be thought of as the chains our moral pilgrim must shed in his or her difficult journey out of Plato's cave of shadows toward an eventually sustained *look* at the Good, the Beautiful, or God.

Augustine begins his description of evil with a rejection of the Manichaean belief in the power of darkness as a force in opposition to God, calling such a view itself evil because of the confusion it causes over whether God is corruptible or incorruptible (*Conf.* VII. 2).[21] He then searches for an alternative explanation for evil and struggles to understand one he has been given, namely, "we do evil because we

---

19. G. R. Evans, *Augustine on Evil* (Cambridge: Cambridge University Press, 1982), 29.
20. Ibid., 32–33.
21. It is important to note his argument with the Manichaeans over who is included in the community of human responsibility because it has historical implications for this project in ecological theology. Augustine rejected the Manichaean view that humans participate in a wider community of living beings that includes all of nature, from animals to rocks. In their view animals are capable of suffering, trees feel pain when cut, etc. Augustine argued that it is only rational minds to whom/which humanity is ethically responsible. The implications of his victory in the debate are enormous, yet complex to trace as we consider today this question of human responsibility in light of the ecological crisis. See Margaret Miles, "Who is 'We': Augustine's Debate with the Manicheans," *Sewanee Theological Review* 41 (Christmas 1997): 34–47.

choose to do so of our own free will, and suffer it because your justice rightly demands that we should" (*Conf.* VII. 3). He affirms that he has a will and then tries to discover why he sometimes acts against that will. Who put such a will in him? If it was the devil, how did the devil come to possess an evil will, if the devil was created by God who is Sweetness itself? He proceeds through and rejects a series of possible explanations for how evil might have stolen into the world, including astrology and the idea that evil exists because of some kind of gap in creation, and he experiences great anxiety that he will die before figuring out the problem of evil (*Conf.* VII. 5-7). Augustine has difficulty communicating the depth of his struggle to his friends, but he takes comfort in the fact that God is listening and hears his suffering. He writes beautifully that God understands his desperate search for a place to rest, for a refuge from the all-consuming challenge of the question of evil (*Conf.* VII. 7).

Augustine then describes his encounter with "some of the books of the Platonists" (*Conf.* VII. 9), and finds an argument that is remarkably similar to the prologue to John's Gospel. He essentially adopts a Platonic return to his own self for the answer to his question, finding an imperishable God, or Plato's dazzling realm of forms, filtered through the New Testament and the incarnation. He searches his soul and finds an unearthly light within; he is amazed at his discovery of the success of a different faculty of perception. "I might more easily have doubted that I was alive than that Truth had being" (*Conf.* VII. 10). He next moves into an aesthetic argument based on the orders of creation, claiming that from God's perspective, evil does not exist (*Conf.* VII. 13). With a God's-eye view, what appears to us to be at odds with the goodness of creation really is not. Augustine catches a glimpse of the world from this perspective, and writes: "I no longer wished for a better world, because I was thinking of the whole of creation, and in light of this clearer discernment I had come to see that though the higher things are better than the lower, the sum of all creation is better than the higher things alone." (*Conf.* VII. 13)

Thus what appears to be evil from our limited perspective is actually a fitting part of the created order from God's perspective, and this is understood through a process of internal examination to achieve right vision. (More on vision below.) Interestingly, he uses examples of what appears to be evil in the natural world, e.g., hail. His argument might be stronger if he had used examples of moral or social, not natural evil. It is perhaps more difficult to understand moral evil than natural disasters or weather as a fitting part of creation.[22]

He then offers a succinct definition of evil. "I saw that it [evil] was not a substance but perversion of the will" (*Conf.* VII. 16). We now have the twofold sense that evil is a function of the improper orientation of an individual will and that evil does not really exist (metaphysically, though it functions as real in an existential sense). Augustine's answer to the problem of evil in this text, then, is a kind of aesthetic optimism: that evil, when properly seen, is nothing but a will that is turned away from God. He is a Platonist with Christian piety on this question, for Christ is the mediator who allows an individual to redirect her will, to survive the moral rigor and training to see clearly (*Conf.* VII. 17). Margaret Miles suggests that Augustine finds a solution to the problem of evil in the Platonists' books, but that he is unsatisfied until he adds the incarnation.[23] The journey out of the cave of shadows is possible (and less lonely perhaps) since the Word was made flesh and dwelt among us. Once he has reached this

[handwritten margin note: Evil = will turned away from God]

---

22. For an excellent exploration of what might be called eco-theodicy, or the question of evil in nature, see Christopher Southgate, *The Groaning of Creation: God, Evolution, and the Problem of Evil* (Louisville: Westminster John Knox, 2008).

23. Margaret Miles, *Desire and Delight: A New Reading of Augustine's Confessions* (New York: Crossroad, 1991), 30.

understanding, the question of the proper orientation of the will to achieve right vision becomes central for Augustine.

Augustine's Use of Physical Vision as a Model

In the ancient world eyes were active, not passive. From Plato, Augustine understands that the mind sends out a ray of light through the eyes toward an object, and the ray touches that object. The person and the object are connected by this ray of light, with the person's will in cooperation. Eventually the object is printed on the soul of that person, and this is how knowledge is gained. A good statement of this theory of vision comes from Plato in his creation story, *Timaeus*:

> The pure fire inside of us flows through our eyes. . . . Now whenever daylight surrounds the visual stream, like makes contact with like and coalesces with it to make up a single homogeneous body aligned with the direction of the eyes. This happens whenever the internal fire strikes and presses against an external object it has connected with. And because this body of fire has become uniform throughout and thus uniformly affected, it transmits the motions of whatever it comes in contact with as well as of whatever comes in contact with it, to and through the whole body until they reach the soul. This brings about the sensation we call "seeing."[24]

Augustine applies this physical model of seeing to his understanding of spiritual vision. He speaks of knowledge from all the senses but assigns priority to vision as the superior sense. "Let us, therefore, rely principally on the testimony of the eyes, for this sense of the body far excels the rest, and comes closer to spiritual vision, though it differs from it in kind."[25] There is a unity between the form that is seen and the viewer (as its image gets pressed on the sense of vision and the

24. Plato, *Timaeus*, trans. with introduction by Donald J. Zeyl (Indianapolis: Hackett, 2000), 33.
25. Augustine, *De trinitate*, trans. Stephen McKenna (Boston: St. Paul Editions, 1965), 204.

will of the soul directs the sense to stay fixed upon it), and then there is no longer any diversity of substance between the viewer and what is seen. He then distinguishes the eye of the body and the eye of the mind, noting later that the human will is what unites them:

> For there are two visions, one of perception, the other of thought. But in order that this vision of thought may be brought about, something similar to it is wrought for this purpose in the memory from the vision of perception, to which the eye of the mind may turn itself in thinking in the same way, as the glance of the eyes turns itself in perceiving to the body.[26]

Thus, though there are limits to the metaphor of vision when used for knowledge of God, there seems to be a continuity between the physical and spiritual vision more than a real difference in kind.

Since the ultimate goal of spiritual sight is to see God face to face, Augustine ruminates on finding vestiges of the Trinity in the world around, including in the beauty of creation, and then in the human soul. It should be noted that such vision requires love in addition to intensive preparation, cleansing, and cultivation/training, as it is difficult to attain.[27] At the end of the journey, in the fulfillment of the resurrection, physical and spiritual vision will be identical. Until that sustained gaze upon God, physical sight offers partial glimpses of a spiritual reality. It is through this lens, the metaphor of physical vision, that Augustine experiences the beautiful in creation as he wrestles with the question of theodicy. In keeping with Plato's proverb, the achievement of a vision of divine beauty is an advanced state for the moral pilgrim, requiring first that one cultivate one's ability to see the higher beauty.

---

26. Ibid., 211.
27. Margaret R. Miles, "Vision: The Eye of the Body and the Eye of the Mind in Saint Augustine's *De trinitate* and *Confessions*," *Journal of Religion* 63 (April 1983): 125–42, at 133.

The Aesthetic Theme of Number in Relation to Vision, or Knowledge Generally that Begins with Sensory Input.

As in the *Timaeus*, number plays a key role in Augustine's aesthetics and is related to the vision model. Like Plato, Augustine believed that numbers were beautiful, conveying the heart of the great theory of beauty above. We understand the nature of numbers in this order of planes:

physical (sensory) →	intellectual (thought and memory) →	innate (judgment of the soul by means of a harmony bestowed upon it by God).[28]

This can be seen clearly in Augustine's *De musica*: "The mind is raised from the consideration of changeable numbers in inferior things to unchangeable numbers in unchangeable truth itself."[29] He discusses meter and rhythm at length, and then in Book 6 he considers music in its cosmological and theological aspects. Just as an experience of the beautiful leads, through the arduous cultivation of spiritual vision, to divine Beauty, so too do numbers of a lower order raise our minds to an unchanging reality that is eternal. Augustine is particularly interested in the beauty, order, and harmony of the whole, as seen in his aesthetic argument regarding the problem of evil, and though we cannot grasp that whole under our fallen state, numbers (proportionality, measure, rhythm, etc.) help us to raise our minds toward it.

> We have recalled . . . that all this is done by God's Providence He has created and rules all things through, so even the sinful and miserable soul

28. Hofstadter, *Philosophies,* 173.
29. Augustine, *De musica,* in *The Fathers of the Church,* v. 4, trans. R. Catesby Taliaferro (Washington, DC: Catholic University of America Press, 1947), 333.

may be moved by numbers and set numbers moving even to the lowest corruption of the flesh. And these numbers can be less and less beautiful, but they can't lack beauty entirely. But God, most good and most just, grudges no beauty whether fashioned by the soul's damnation, retreat, or perseverance. But number also begins from one, and is beautiful in equality and likeness, and bound by order.[30]

Again we see the themes of order, beauty that is eternal, and the finite leading the pilgrim closer to the infinite, unchanging reality. A glimpse of God's beauty can be discerned in number, weight, and measure on this side of eternal life. The beauty of numbers—alongside the cultivation of vision—thus plays a key role in Augustine's aesthetics.

Beauty and Resurrected Life

It is often said that *The City of God* should be read backwards, beginning with Augustine's vision of resurrected life and then moving back through how he understands mortal life on this side of heaven. He provides a vision, a fantasy of resurrection that involves the completion and perfection of human beings. He offers a vision of the resurrected human body intact, sexually differentiated in the interest of beauty, and free from the perils of lust. So while human fulfillment is postponed to the next life and this life is punishment for humanity's state after the fall, there is a *telos* for Augustine that is glorious and deeply connected to his aesthetics.

To our modern and postmodern ears and eyes his *City of God* can be deeply disturbing for its insistence that while we live in a city on a pilgrimage to that heavenly city of life after death we are to maintain the social and political status quo (note: this text was written against the backdrop of the sack of Rome). Yet this work should be

30. Ibid., 375.

read with the final book as a lens through which to view the rest. For Augustine, we are headed for a fully glorious humanity in the resurrection, in which the eyes of the body and the spiritual eyes share the same vision. He sees finite glimpses now (*imago Dei*) in our present human nature.

Interestingly, seeing natural beauty has an important role in his vision, both as consolation for this pilgrim life on earth and as a foretaste of God's greater blessings to come:

> Then there is the beauty and utility of the natural creation, which the divine generosity has bestowed on man, for him to behold and to take into use, even though mankind has been condemned and cast out from paradise into the hardships and miseries of this life. How could any description do justice to all these blessings? The manifold diversity of beauty in the sky and earth and sea; the abundance of light, and its miraculous loveliness, in sun and moon and stars; the dark shades of woods, the color and fragrance of flowers; the multitudinous varieties of birds, with their songs and their bright plumage . . . . Who could give a complete list of all these natural blessings?
>
> . . . And these are all the consolations of mankind under condemnation, not the rewards of the blessed. What then will those rewards be, if the consolations are so many and so wonderful? What will God give to those whom he has predestined to life, if he has given all these to those predestined to death? (*City of God* XXII. 24)

In the early church the influence of Greek thought made achieving a vision of beauty a central motif of early Christian aesthetics. Beauty, in the natural world or art or numbers, had the power to elevate human perception nearer to divine reality. This elevation, the result of arduous cultivation and divine assistance, constituted the hope of the faithful while on earth. Natural beauty could be seen as a kind of stepping stone to a higher beauty, though that beauty could not be reached in its fullness under the conditions of mortal life. Augustine drew on Plato's optimism for the human journey out of the cave of shadows, but stopped short of the actual achievement of the highest vision. Natural beauty takes on the role not only of stepping stone, but of a comforting vestige of heavenly beauty yet to come. It could stir the soul and help it reach a proper orientation: away from evil and toward the holy. In short, according to the broad and meticulous foundation laid by Augustine of Hippo for subsequent Christian aesthetics, beauty could bring us closer to God and thus is salvific, but we must wait until the resurrection for the highest beauty and human fulfillment.

The Medieval Church: The Grasp of Beauty

According to Umberto Eco, beauty in the medieval world was understood metaphysically as intelligible—a religious, moral, and psychological reality. Philosophers and mystics were enthralled with luminosity and with the manifestation or emanation of God seen in the world around. There was a sense of urgency to understand beauty and its lessons, an urgency that went hand in hand with a genuine sense of melancholy during the Middle Ages about the transience of earthly beauty and human life. Life and beauty slipped quickly away, and the challenge was to grasp that beauty as it did so.

Interestingly, such beauty was not to be confused with art, though there were parallels. In particular, in the interest of grasping metaphysical beauty people were often suspicious of too much ornate, human-created beauty in churches since it could distract the worshipers. Thomas Aquinas argued, for example (as the reformer Zwingli, a trained musician, would later), that instrumental music should not be used in the Mass since acute pleasure from such music would divert worshipers' attention from a higher focus. Beyond such artistic distractions and iconoclastic impulses, however, the medieval world looked to a beauty that could teach metaphysically and allegorically if grasped. Symbolically, the hand of God could be discerned in the beauty of the world, and allegorically the world itself could be perceived as a divine work of art, in which everything contained in the world promised moral, allegorical, and analogical meanings.[31] Thus within the guiding question of the medieval church about the relationship between transient earthly beauty and attaining salvific knowledge or understanding of God we may look to three theologians—Hildegard of Bingen, Bonaventure, and Thomas Aquinas—for insights on how to grasp beauty in this earthly life.

Hildegard of Bingen (1098–1179) was an extraordinary twelfth-century abbess: visionary, prophet, preacher, composer, and mystic. She studied and wrote about theology, medicine, and mental and physical diseases, completing six books and the first known Christian morality play. She founded monasteries, traveled widely, maintained extensive correspondence, and achieved fame in her own lifetime. Within all these roles and accomplishments she understood herself as an instrument of God, playing in a cosmic symphony.

To understand Hildegard in her own context, we can look to a twelfth-century renaissance of sorts. There was a renewed interest in miracles. The doctrine of purgatory was being developed. There was a new attentiveness to the natural world and its order and laws, and importantly, a new curiosity about the unity between the natural and supernatural worlds. The search was on for an understanding of an integrated order. A focus on Hildegard the composer's theology of music in particular will demonstrate this search clearly and provide a helpful lens through which to explore the question of her

---

31. Umberto Eco, *Art and Beauty in the Middle Ages* (New Haven: Yale University Press, 1986), Introduction and chap. 1.

understanding of the relationship between grasping beauty in the created world and knowledge of God.

Hildegard's contemporaries heard her music and called it beautiful and strange.[32] Her wide range and strenuous melodic leaps (or *melismata*, which are long, wide-ranging musical phrases sung on a single vowel sound) were innovative. We know that she understood her music to be a reflection of the angelic liturgy that is happening continuously, claiming that her compositions (as well as her visions) came to her through direct revelation from God. Music, for Hildegard, was intended solely for a liturgical setting, and in that context it has the power to raise our senses to divine realities, which are themselves musical. She makes several metaphorical connections between music and knowledge of God: the peace of heaven is a celestial harmony and the human soul is symphonic, especially when it praises God through music.[33] Vocal music functioned directly, it seems, as a bridge between humanity and the divine realm, transporting singers and hearers alike.

In 1178, when an interdict against singing the daily office was imposed after the burial of a formerly excommunicated nobleman on abbey grounds, Hildegard had to come up with an apology for the necessity of music. She obeyed the interdict while protesting it in every way she could. Interestingly, historian Barbara Newman suggests that she seemed more upset about the silencing of chant than about the other penalties.[34] In one of her arguments for being allowed to sing again we find a statement of her theology of music. She wrote that before Adam's fall, his holy voice had rung "with the sound of every harmony and the sweetness of the whole art of music.

---

32. Margaret R. Miles, in a lecture at the Graduate Theological Union, December 4, 2002.

33. Robert Boenig, "Music and Mysticism in Hildegard's *O ignis spiritus paracliti*," *Studia Mystica* 9, no. 3 (Fall 1986): 60–72.

34. Barbara Newman, ed. *Voice of the Living Light: Hildegard of Bingen and Her World* (Berkeley: University of California Press, 1998), 27–28.

And if he had remained in the condition in which he was formed, human frailty could never endure the power and the resonance of his voice."[35] She was quick to note that Satan lures "humankind away from the celestial harmony" and cannot bear to hear music. So with the interdict the prelates were doing the devil's work by silencing the nuns and depriving God of the praise God deserves.

Another good source for discerning Hildegard's theology of music is in her vision, *Scivia* 25, "The Communion of Saints in Cosmic Symphony," in which we learn that humanity has two functions: singing praise to God and doing good works. In this vision she meditates on how we on earth enter into communion with the saints by way of music.

> Through the power of hearing, God opens to human beings all the glorious sounds of the hidden mysteries and of the choirs of angels by whom God is praised over and over again. It would be unfitting if God could not be recognized in the same manner that one person recognizes another, namely by his or her hearing powers. Indeed, here human beings from within their own selves, come to an understanding of the whole. We would be empty were we not able to hear and comprehend.[36]

For her, communion is inconceivable without hearing music. Our "understanding of the whole" or cosmological unity happens this way.[37] One could summarize her theology of music as follows: God is music and creation sings God's praise, and knowledge of God or communion with God is acquired through participating in this heavenly music.

---

35. Ibid.

36. Matthew Fox, *Illuminations of Hildegard of Bingen* (Santa Fe: Bear & Co., 1985), 25–26.

37. I do not mean to suggest in this treatment that Hildegard prioritized hearing and singing over other sense perceptions or finding beauty in creation in other ways, but I am treating her theology of music as indicative of how she understood uniting with God through beauty. Just as Augustine emphasized vision as a metaphor for gaining spiritual understanding, Hildegard prioritizes the sense of hearing.

The most important point, for Hildegard, is that music is creation "rebounding to the celestial Creator with a single voice of exultation and joy and the giving of thanks." Music is the way to give thanks to God. The whole universe makes music from its harmonious interconnection. "All of creation is a song of praise to God."[38] And, importantly, we are sanctified by joining our voices in that song. The human soul and creation work in concert to create a symphony. The chorus of the communion of saints integrates itself into the greater chorus of the cosmos itself. By extension, it is the devil's work to disrupt the beauty and joy of music. Interestingly, Hildegard blames Satan, not Eve, for destroying the original divine-human harmony. Music clearly has a soteriological significance for Hildegard the composer, as it helps us to grasp cosmic and divine beauty.

Moving from music specifically to the beauty of creation generally, as regards the question of natural beauty in relation to knowledge of God, there is a relevant term that seems to be Hildegard's own innovation. That term is *viriditas*, loosely translated as the "greening power" of God. She uses it to describe the exquisite greening of trees and grasses, the earth's lush greening. All of creation and humanity in particular is "showered with greening refreshment, the vitality to bear fruit." Creativity and greening power are intimately connected. "Greening love hastens to the aid of all. With the passion of heavenly yearning, people who breathe this dew produce rich fruit."[39]

Christ brings lush greenness to shriveled and wilted people or institutions. Redemption involves moisture, almost like being reconstituted after dehydration. The Word of God is all verdant greening, all creativity. Hildegard calls God "the purest spring." The Holy Spirit is greening power in motion, making all things grow, expand, celebrate. Salvation or healing is the return of greening

38. Ibid., 26.
39. Ibid., xiii.

power and moistness, a return to the fullness before the fall (read: before withering). If we think back to how Satan is responsible for the fall, and how Satan has no song in him, there is an interesting connection between *viriditas*, nature imagery, music, and salvation. Hildegard seems to have understood and expressed the kind of cosmological unity that medieval people sought, with beauty in the natural world playing a key allegorical role.

In one of Hildegard's compositions, *O viridissima virga*, we see the vibrancy of her nature imagery intertwined with her theological convictions. In the center of the piece the Virgin's womb brings forth the earthly material for the Eucharist as well as the Word of God. In the whole work Mary is likened to the tree of Jesse from the book of Isaiah, pointing to the ancestry of Christ. She uses the tree image as a symbol that connects earth (the Hebrew scriptures) and heaven (New Testament revelation). Mary is the greenest branch, the one with the lifegiving greening power of heaven. We see salvation history being played out through nature imagery, undoubtedly reflective of the landscape of her home in the Rhineland-Palatinate region of what is now Germany, as everything becomes replenished in its freshness.

Hildegard's compositions and *Scivias* (both text and illustrations, whether or not the illustrations may be properly attributed to her) are infused with a sense of joy and a profound optimism and trust that human souls and creation are in a symphony together, a chorus in communion. Beauty is a kind of bridge between humanity and God, and we can find ourselves on that bridge through music as well as the natural beauty around us created by God. Her concept of *viriditas,* especially her hope in the regenerative power of God, is a powerful idea for ecological theology today. But what she accomplished in her own day was an understanding of a cosmic unity between humanity and the divine with beauty as the link. Beauty thus could be grasped and could allow for a harmonious communion with God.

Bonaventure (ca. 1217–1274), a second founder of the Franciscan order, followed a different trajectory from that of Francis of Assisi. While Francis focused on an incarnational perspective in which the sensible world provided a form for contemplation and an arena for the activity of God's holiness, Bonaventure took a more hierarchical and intellectualized view. They answered the nominalism/realism question of what is ultimately real—categories or things, for example, Beauty or the beautiful that is experienced—in different ways, though perhaps they should be understood as having two different emphases rather than a real difference in kind. Bonaventure's understanding of this issue can be seen in his *The Mind's Road to God* and is directly related to the question of the relationship between grasping beauty in the natural world and knowledge of God.

Francis never quite condemned academic learning, but he did not endorse it as a worthy primary activity for a disciple. Bonaventure, on the other hand, taught at the University of Paris and reinterpreted Francis's view of learning. In a sense he replaced Francis's physical asceticism with rigorous study and an intellectual asceticism. What Francis lived and felt, Bonaventure intellectualized and thought, so that what is ultimately real can be grasped through a series of abstractions.[40] A prime example of this is the way he translated Francis's vision of the six-winged seraph that gave him the stigmata into six steps of meditation as the mind's road to God:

Sense →Imagination →Reason →Intellect →Intelligence →Illumination

40. Miles, *The Word Made Flesh*, 162–64.

In terms of the question of the relationship between beauty in the natural world and knowledge of God, the body and the sensible world hold the ambiguous honor of being the starting point of this six-step ladder to God. A quality of attentiveness to the natural world is required on the first rung of the ladder. A key ingredient for success at the beginning of the journey is the experience of delight in the natural world; this delight provides energy for the rest of the ascent to God, or the ultimate delight. Drawing directly on Augustine's *De musica* (Book VI), Bonaventure writes:

> Therefore, since all things are beautiful and in some way delightful, and since beauty and delight do not exist without proportion, and since proportion exists primarily in numbers, all things are subject to numbers. Hence, number is the principal vestige leading to Wisdom. And since number is most evident to all and very close to God, it leads us, by its sevenfold distinction, very close to Him; it makes Him known in all bodily and visible things when we apprehend numerical things, when we delight in numerical proportions, and when we judge irrefutably by the laws of numerical proportions.[41]

Thus Bonaventure shares Augustine's aesthetic understanding of number and proportion and his (neo-Platonic) view that knowledge of God begins with knowledge of the sensible world and results from a process of abstraction/ascent from there. He shares with Aristotle and Thomas Aquinas a sense of delight in that process. What is beautiful in the natural world (in this case, beauty that demonstrates proportionality) pleases, and it fuels the journey.

As seen in the first chapter of *The Mind's Road to God*, pilgrims are required to look within, since this journey is innate (as is the knowledge of God at the end of the road), and then to look more deeply *through* the sensible world as the first step on the journey.

---

41. Bonaventure, *The Mind's Road to God*, trans. Philotheus Boehner (Indianapolis: Hackett, 1956), 16.

From all this, one can gather that since the creation of the world his invisible attributes are clearly seen, being understood through the things that are made. And so they are without excuse who are unwilling to take notice of these things, or to know, bless, and love God in them, since they are unwilling to be transported out of darkness into the marvelous light of God. But thanks be to God through our Lord, Jesus Christ, Who has transported us out of darkness into his marvelous light, since by these lights externally given, we are disposed to reenter the mirror of our mind, wherein shine forth divine things.[42]

What makes the place of the natural world and its beauty in this path somewhat ambiguous is that the pilgrim ultimately leaves it behind for a higher and *internal* level of abstraction. Because of this, Bonaventure is often read as a kind of anti-body, anti-world theologian. However, I would argue that this is something of a misinterpretation. The rungs of the ladder of ascent are not exactly progressive stages of abstraction in which previous steps are disregarded in favor of those ahead. Rather, they are distilled together in a sense, as *reductio*: "While you consider these things, one by one, you have the subject matter that lifts you to the utmost heights of admiration. Therefore, that your mind may rise, through admiration, to admiring contemplation, *you must consider all these attributes together*."[43]

Francis's six steps are certainly a hierarchical ladder for Bonaventure. Keeping all the rungs together yields the unified vision of God at the top of the ladder. Beauty in the natural world is the start of the journey to contemplation of God. It provides delight, and a lens through which divine things can shine. The journey requires arduous cultivation of spiritual vision, as understood by Augustine centuries before. At the end of the journey, Francis's ecstasy becomes

42. Ibid., 17.
43. Ibid., 35. Emphasis supplied. See also Miles, *The Word Made Flesh*, 162–64.

Bonaventure's wonder. In short, Francis showed his followers the way of the body while Bonaventure offered the way of the mind, a kind of discursive mapping of Francis's vision. Thomas Aquinas would seek a third way that would integrate body and intellectual order.

To return briefly to Bonaventure's writing about Francis's vision of the winged seraph and receiving the stigmata, we should note that an important element of Bonaventure's aesthetics can be seen here. Hans Urs von Balthasar discusses Bonaventure's understanding of the aesthetics of form.[44] Karl Rahner and others have read Francis's experience of the seraph as an ecstatic, apophatic mystical experience. Bonaventure, on the other hand, focuses not on perception of the stigmata but on the active impression that the form of the beautiful makes upon Francis. He uses the image of warm wax, for example, to describe how the beautiful presses upon one and leaves a lasting impression. Form imprints itself, and this experience is succeeded by contemplation of the form. One of the consequences of this different angle on Francis's experience is that the form of the beautiful acquires a kind of objectivity, though it is important to note that the one who experiences this is also engaged on a subjective level. So, rather than focusing on passive perception of the beautiful, Bonaventure would say that our senses are shaped by the beautiful through its active impression upon us. An indirect parallel could be drawn here to the ancient understanding of vision discussed above in which sight creates an active connection, not a passive perception.

In light of this understanding, how should we read the end of the journey in *The Mind's Road to God*? Is that end to be found in a mystical experience that is beyond the senses, or is it mystical as well

---

44. Hans Urs Von Balthasar, *The Glory of the Lord: A Theological Aesthetics, II: Studies in Theological Style: Clerical Styles* (San Francisco: Ignatius Press, 1984), 260–360. I am also drawing on lecture notes from Alejandro Garcia-Rivera's theological aesthetics course at the Graduate Theological Union, October 29, 2002.

as aesthetic in some sense—in Bonaventure's understanding of the aesthetic as being not just passive perception but a kind of touching or ontological shaping of the pilgrim? It seems that for Bonaventure aesthetics is not about mimesis, the visible pointing as a sign to the invisible, but rather is the invisible making form visible. There is a sense of being grasped by beauty in an aesthetic experience that is also a religious experience, and this is a view shared by Thomas Aquinas.

Bonaventure and Hildegard share an understanding that the grasp of natural beauty assists us in our quest for knowledge of God. For Hildegard, participation in created beauty transports us to a heavenly realm. For Bonaventure, the journey is less direct, less immediate. It requires abstraction from earthly beauty and a more nuanced take on how the experience of the beautiful shapes us *en route*. I now turn to the aesthetics of Thomas Aquinas, who takes Bonaventure's abstraction of beauty in a different direction with the introduction of analogy into his theological method.

Thomas Aquinas (ca. 1225–1274) taught at the University of Paris at a time when Aristotle's works had recently arrived in the West, in the twelfth century, largely through Muslim commentaries. With them came a new kind of empirical attention paid to the natural world and an understanding that knowledge comes from the senses. There were fierce debates about the proper use of Aristotle, who was seen at the time as a godless philosopher who analyzed the world without God, or perhaps with the divine as an ambiguous first cause. Thomas inherited this complex question of the relationship between God and the natural world. He ultimately changed the ontological question of the relationship of God to the world (how being is distributed) to an epistemological question (how humanity can know being). So while Bonaventure saw the world as access or as the first step for intellectual ascent in a kind of synthesis between subjectivity and empiricism, Thomas developed a more subtle approach. He distinguished philosophy (reason) from theology (faith), though they are not discontinuous. The rational mind is the perfect vehicle to know the sensible world (thus Aristotle), but this is not the right tool for understanding revelation. Faith is the proper instrument for that. Interestingly, Thomas was the first to separate theology and scriptural exegesis, a huge innovation. His task was to understand the connection between faith and reason, which he found in the method of analogy. He then went on to draw out the analogies between nature and faith.[45]

Thomas was careful to define the limits of analogy in theological method and the use of the process of negation. One cannot prove by analogy, for example. Analogies suggest, enable, illuminate, but knowledge of God is by grace.

> We know incorporeal realities, which have no sense images, by analogy with sensible bodies, which do have images, just as we understand truth in the abstract by a consideration of things in which we see truth. God we know, according to Dionysius, as cause about which we ascribe the utmost perfection and negate any limit. Furthermore, we cannot, in our present state, know other incorporeals except negatively and by analogy with corporeal realities. Thus, when we understand anything of these beings, we necessarily have to turn to images of sensible things.[46]

Thus images are necessary for theology. In order to answer the question about the relationship between beauty in the natural world and knowledge of God, Thomas would explore such beauty as analogy. Unlike Bonaventure and Hildegard, he would distinguish what can be known of the natural world through philosophy from what can be known by revelation, rejecting a simple kind of

---

45. Miles, *The Word Made Flesh*, chaps. 3 and 4.
46. Thomas Aquinas, *Summa Theologiae* Ia, 84, 8 ad 3.

cosmological continuum between what we see and experience in this world and the divine realm.

In terms of aesthetics, Thomas distinguishes between essence and existence generally, and specifically between beauty and the beautiful. This distinction will endure through the modern period and into the present day. Beauty, according to Thomas, is the cause of the beautiful in the realm of experience, and he asserts that the beautiful participates in divine or transcendent beauty, rather than reflecting it as a mirror. This is a key difference between Thomas and the two theologians referenced above. The starting point of aesthetics will necessarily be corporeal beauty, experienced on the sensory, empirical plane. But transcendent beauty cannot be known directly in this way; it can only be grasped rationally through analogy on what von Balthasar calls the superessential level.[47]

In Thomas's aesthetics the beautiful is something the grasp (*apprehensio*) of which pleases. In the Middle Ages the love of beauty went hand in hand with a fear of beauty that could manipulate human emotions, as Eco suggests. Thomas offers a deeper understanding of aesthetic pleasure beyond mere gratification. Pleasure in the beautiful is a kind of insight into a higher realm of essence, transcending this realm of experience.[48] As for Augustine, this pleasure has to do with human fulfillment, not just a fleeting joy or happiness in the experience of the beautiful.

Thomas suggests that there are three conditions of the beautiful: *proportio*, *integritas*, and *claritas*. His understanding of proportion is similar to that of Augustine, Bonaventure, and others, as a kind of fitness of parts within a whole. *Integritas* is a kind of organic wholeness, a unity in variety. *Claritas* is an idea that Thomas

---

47. Hans Urs Von Balthasar, *The Glory of the Lord: A Theological Aesthetics, IV: The Realm of Metaphysics in Antiquity* (San Francisco: Ignatius Press, 1989), 407.
48. Alejandro Garcia-Rivera, course lecture GTU, 11/12/02.

essentially derives from Pseudo-Dionysius, adding a different understanding of being so as not to fall into a kind of inadvertent pantheism: God is the cause of *claritas* in that God lets things participate in God's own primal light. We experience *claritas* through the senses, given the intelligibility of form, though this is not Bonaventure's "imprint." We can see concretely through *claritas* the existence of the reality of beauty, even if we cannot grasp beauty fully through the intellect.[49]

Thomas offers a theological method for aesthetics that explores the possibility of the objectivity of beauty as a transcendental while taking into account subjective conditions for its experience. He thus provides a bridge to the modern period as he differentiates between philosophy/reason, revelation/faith, and concrete human experience. While Hildegard and Bonaventure saw divine beauty directly mirrored in the beauty of creation, Thomas turns to the experience of the beautiful as an opportunity to gain rational insight into the realm of divine beauty through analogy. Divine beauty, in a sense, has become much more complex to define by the time we get to Thomas. As von Balthasar writes, "Finally, it must be remembered that there can objectively be no 'definition' of the transcendentals, just as being itself is indefinable."[50] Plato understood early that beautiful things are difficult. The medieval church discovered the first glimpses of more specific roadblocks in the attempt to grasp beauty, challenges that would only increase in the coming centuries.

Reformation: The Suspicion of Beauty

Wladyslaw Tatarkiewicz describes the Renaissance as a key turning point in views of art, artists, and beauty. Before this, art and beauty

49. Von Balthasar, *Metaphysics in Antiquity*, 408, 410.
50. Ibid., 411.

had been separate in a sense, and the Renaissance brought a new kind of approximation of art and beauty. With the advent of secular humanism and corresponding cultural shifts, including a new exploration of the authority of the artist (now a visionary, no longer an anonymous craftsman) and the artist's creativity, works of art for the first time became the vehicle for conveying metaphysical beauty. A key innovation of the era was that metaphysical ideals were now to be found within the artist, to be drawn out in a work of art. Attention had been turned from the beauty of the world to the beauty of art as that which can convey metaphysical truth/reality. The fine arts as such were born, human creativity had a new prominence, and individual artists were recognized by name for the first time. In the history of Western art, Romanticism was just around the corner. Such tremendous shifts in the world of art paved the way for what Tatarkiewicz calls a crisis in the great theory of beauty that comes with the modern period, a shift in which we move from an appreciation of the greatness of beauty that transcends individuals to witnessing its gradual decline on the artistic and philosophical landscape.[51] This decline would see its fullest expression beginning in the eighteenth century and moving into the twentieth.

While the Renaissance took flight and modern sensibilities were born, and the great theory of beauty began its decline, the winds of religious reform swept across Europe and iconoclastic debates were renewed with fervor. Music and visual art were highly suspect, for they had the power to distract and even tempt the faithful away from God. Churches were stripped of art as pulpits rose in prominence as a symbol of the Reformation emphasis on the priority of the Word of God over all else. In this context one might expect that the trajectory we have been tracing of the role of natural beauty

51. Tartarkiewicz, *History of Ideas*, 127–28.

in relation to divine knowledge would cower under philosophical and religious pressure and come to a halt. Surprisingly, the story continues, albeit in a quieter mode, among early modern theologians. With the consuming emphasis on the means of conversion and sanctification of the reform movements of the sixteenth century we find a role for natural beauty in relation to soteriology, as seen in the work of John Calvin and Jonathan Edwards. Each appeals to the Christian's experience of natural beauty, though their work is tempered by the limits of the trustworthiness of individual experiences in a bewildering world filled with sin and grace.

John Calvin (1509–1564), a second-generation Reformer, wrote *The Institutes of Christian Religion* to aid Christians with right instruction at a time when French Protestants were under persecution. He wrote the work for all Christians, appealing for tolerance in a time of great strife. In his overarching theological vision Calvin was concerned with recognizing, maintaining, and preserving the glory of God, a concern that informed everything he wrote. The pressing question for him, undoubtedly connected to the turmoil and violence of religious differences, is why we do not see God's glory and our own corruption more clearly.[52]

In order to explore the role of natural beauty in his primary concerns with conversion and sanctification, let us begin with a brief overview of those processes in Calvin's system. Before conversion we are sluggish, drowsy, and lethargic, and we do not see the glory of God or our own sinfulness. Then there is a moment of "quickening" in which one recognizes an intimate connection between the believer and Christ—as bread becomes fuel for the body, so Christ enables one to see God's activity in the world. With quickening there is a need to adjust our vision to the speed of the reality of our total

---

52. Miles, *The Word Made Flesh*, 268–70.

depravity, a key religious theme throughout Calvin's system. It is as if the rug is pulled out from under us and we begin to fall. The proper response to this moment of awakening/falling, according to Calvin, is faith, which comes with an instant participation in the fullness of God. Sanctification, in turn, is the process of translating this quickening moment into repentance for our failures and inadequacy and gratitude for a new life in Christ; this process happens over a lifetime. Calvin believed that self-knowledge and knowledge of God are thus intimately connected.[53]

In terms of natural beauty on the journey of sanctification, Calvin insisted that the glory of God can be known in creation, where evidence of the Creator can be seen in beauty and goodness. Creation sings praise to the Creator, which we can hear if we open our senses:

> In every part of the world in heaven and on earth he has written and engraven the glory of his power, goodness, wisdom, and eternity. Truly as St. Paul said the Lord never left himself without a witness, even to those to whom he has sent no knowledge of his word. For all creatures, even from the firmament to the center of the earth, could be witnesses and messengers of his glory to all people. For the little singing birds sang of God; the animals acclaimed him; the elements feared and the mountains resounded with him; the rivers and springs threw glances toward him; the flowers and the grasses smiled. So that in truth there was no need to seek him afar, seeing that everyone could find God within himself, inasmuch as we are all sustained and preserved by his virtue abiding in us.[54]

Nature thus reveals the glory of God (Calvin's primary concern) and, to a limited extent, knowledge of God, but it is easy to overlook this since we live in a fallen state. We therefore need help from scripture in recognizing the revelation of God in nature:

---

53. Ibid., 270–71.
54. François Wendel, *Calvin: The Origins and Development of His Religious Thought,* trans. Philip Mairet (New York: Harper & Row, 1963), 161.

Therefore, though the effulgence which is presented to every eye, both in the heavens and on the earth, leaves the ingratitude of humanity without excuse, since God, in order to bring the whole human race under the same condemnation, holds forth to all, without exception, a mirror of his deity, in his works, another and better help must be given to guide us properly to God as a Creator. Not in vain, therefore, has he added the light of his word, in order that he might make himself known unto salvation . . . [*Institutes* I. 1]

In Calvin's system the experience of natural beauty accomplishes two things in conversion and sanctification: (1) beauty can provide a platform for the quickening, or conversion process, that precedes sanctification. It does this by showing forth God's glory, which in turn holds our own depravity up to the light of day by comparison so that the extent of our sinfulness can be seen clearly. (2) Beauty in the world also sings praise to God, and with the help of scripture we can see this clearly and join our own voices in that praise. This is part of our sanctification. Our repentance and gratitude for new life in Christ grow over time, and we are able see the evidence of God around us more clearly as God's virtue abiding in us increases.

It should be noted that individual experience as a category has its limits for Calvin, and the experience of natural beauty plays but a small role in his system of conversion and sanctification. Seeing evidence of the Creator's glory is one thing, but Calvin would insist that we are not to go looking for God too closely in natural beauty, for this would reflect human pride. "The right way to seek God and the best rule we can follow is not to force ourselves with too bold a curiosity to inquire into the majesty, which we ought rather to worship than to investigate too curiously, but to contemplate God in his works, by which he renders himself near and familiar to us and, we might say, communicates himself."[55] Rather than investigating

---

55. Jean Calvin, *The Institutes of Christian Religion*, trans. Ford Lewis Battles. LCC 20 (Philadelphia: Westminster Press, 1960), I. 4. 1.

any kind of natural theology or medieval bridge between natural beauty and knowledge of God, a Christian is called to see God's glory communicated through the world around and simply praise God in return.

Jonathan Edwards (1703–1758), a Calvinist clergyman and key figure in the first Great Awakening and one of the most original American philosophers and preachers, had a love of natural beauty and a corresponding aesthetic theme in his writings. Influenced by British empiricism and drawing on John Locke's understanding that God is known indirectly through a mix of reason and experience, Edwards sought to explain the experience of beauty as one that is mediated through the senses, not mystical or apophatic. Experience, in fact, plays a pivotal role in Edwards's aesthetics, and this is an innovation that breaks with European philosophies of beauty at the time. As a Puritan, Edwards shared Calvin's almost singular focus on God's glory expressed in creation, but Edwards asked the question of the *experience* of natural beauty in relation to knowledge of God in a new and surprising way in eighteenth-century New England.[56]

Edwards is perhaps best known for his attention to sensation, both in preaching and in his miscellaneous writings. His sermon, "Sinners in the Hands of an Angry God," has gone down in history as a terrifying and provocative experience of hell and heaven for his hearers and for readers since. Using language carefully, he was able to create experiences for his congregation that brought the theological realities he was trying to convey to tangible life. He was a master of finding language appropriate to the realities he tried to illuminate. Similarly, when reading about the excellence of spiderwebs, lightning, and other natural phenomena in great detail one sees Edwards as a theologian in search of language adequate

56. Miles, *The Word Made Flesh*, 373–74.

enough to convey the sensations he experienced.[57] It is with such quality of attention to sensory detail that he turns to natural beauty as a kind of springboard for how the human heart is moved and comes to deeper knowledge of God.

A central concept in Edwards's aesthetics is that of consent, which, in the process of sanctification, one gives in a sense to natural beauty. There are two kinds of consent, cordial and natural. In natural consent one finds an intellectually agreeable arrangement of proportion in harmony, color, number, scent, etc. This is familiar territory for ancient aesthetics and the great theory of beauty. Through such arrangement one finds beauty in nature. Edwards sees this, for example, in spiderwebs as well as diagrams the human mind can devise (as seen in his "thought experiments"), thus connecting human creativity and natural beauty.

The second kind of consent is cordial, in which the heart and mind become one—understanding and will cease to be separate faculties, the state Augustine longed for—and through sensible knowledge one reaches understanding of a primary Beauty that is divine. There is a trajectory from the first kind of consent to the other, and the steps are as follows:[58]

Consent →	Consent to Being →	Consent of Being to Being →	Cordial Consent of Being to Being →	Cordial Consent of Being to Being in General (this is divine Beauty or Excellency).

One of the best interpretive summaries I have found of Edwards's concepts of Excellency or Beauty and consent is by Richard R. Niebuhr:

---

57. Alejandro Garcia-Rivera, course lecture GTU, 3/11/03.
58. Jonathan Edwards, "The Mind," in *A Jonathan Edwards Reader,* ed. John E. Smith (New Haven: Yale University Press, 1995), 22–34.

We may say that Excellency is Beauty. An excellent being is never one being alone but being-in-relation. Complex Beauty better exhibits Excellency than Simple Beauty, for Complex Beauty often involves particular disproportions or "confusions," which yet contribute to a more universal or inclusive beauty. Natural phenomena, such as flowers, trees, and the human body, as well as sensible perception, exemplify such Complex Beauty. The relations that natural phenomena present to us are relations of agreement. The relations that spiritual beings present to us are relations of consent or love. When pleasure arises in the act of perceiving, it is a sign of the excellence of what is perceived. The more expansive and intense is the system of consents or of love, the more excellent are those beings who participate in that system. This is what Edwards means when he writes, "[For], so far as a thing consents to Being in general, so far it consents to [God]; and the more perfect Created Spirits are, the nearer they come to their Creator, in this regard."[59]

Natural beauty presents proportionality that leads us to an affective understanding of spiritual beauty through a series of consents, or love. There is delight (Thomas's pleasure?) for Edwards in sense perception of beauty in the natural world, which fuels the journey toward cordial consent to being in general. This final consent is consent to God, which is another way of articulating being in the fullest possible relationship to God. Sanctification was a primary concern for Edwards, as it was for Calvin, and it is clear that for Edwards the experience of natural beauty and its splendor are key to the moral and religious life, especially in terms of growing more perfect (having more virtue, more understanding, etc.) in the life of faith.

Sensation, for Edwards, is the path from experience/senses to understanding/idea. Sensory experience clearly plays an essential role. The human will is moved through sensible knowledge, and this must have been liberating for a Calvinist.[60] I do not mean, however,

---

59. Richard R. Niebuhr, "Edwards' Idea of Excellency or Beauty," (unpublished class handout), Harvard Divinity School, September 1997, 12.

to overemphasize the place of individual experience in Edwards's thought. He wrote during a revivalist period that witnessed a fervor (and at times a mania) over the question of election. Hand in hand with the hope for signs of the Spirit came a deep distrust that such signs were indeed from God. Edwards wrote *The Religious Affections* as an attempt to discern and distinguish signs of true conversion and sanctification from false ones. As also for Calvin, experience was not to be trusted naïvely or uncritically.

In both Calvin and Edwards after him we find a place for natural beauty within the life of faith. We also find a turn to the experience of that natural beauty *and* a suspicion of what that beauty can teach that place them squarely in the modern period. Each demonstrates the continuity of theological reflection on natural beauty within soteriology while also illuminating particular difficulties in maintaining that trajectory into the modern period, when beauty comes under suspicion.

Enlightenment: The Apparent Decline of Beauty

With the advent of Enlightenment rationalism our trajectory moves from classically influenced theories of beauty to theorizing about the subjective experience of the beautiful, which Tatarkiewicz calls an eighteenth-century Copernican revolution in aesthetics.[61] He suggests that the great theory of beauty survived more or less intact for twenty-two centuries, from roughly the fifth century B.C.E. through the seventeenth century C.E. It is not until the eighteenth century of our era that beauty begins to be approached in a dramatically different way. Art becomes the purview of philosophy as a third division alongside theoretical and practical knowledge.

60. As suggested by Alejandro Garcia-Rivera, course lecture, GTU, 3/11/03.
61. Tartarkiewicz, *History of Ideas*, 129, 138.

The term "aesthetics" is coined as the science of sensory cognition, or what makes something beautiful, according to Alexander Baumgarten.[62] Interest in the classical (ontological, metaphysical, transcendental, etc.) concept of beauty falls away, while interest in aesthetics increases. In the modern period art becomes a thing of interest to the individual "consumer" of art. What matters is the individual's experience of a work of art.

In his *Critique of Judgment*, Immanuel Kant (1724–1804) launched modern aesthetics and ascribed to the aesthetic sphere a status equal to the theoretical (cognitive) and practical (moral) realms.[63] His project was to explain the validity of judgments of beauty, taste, and sublimity. Moving away from beauty as a transcendental teacher, he declared that all judgments about beauty and taste are individual and result from a mapping of aesthetic experience by *a priori* concepts of the mind. Beauty is that which pleases, neither through impression nor concepts but with subjective necessity in an immediate, universal, and disinterested way. Thus Kant's disinterested observer is a universal figure: all such rational observers will come to the same conclusion about a work of art, which must be beautiful and must satisfy taste. Interestingly, for Kant art can only be called beautiful if we see it as art and yet, at the same time, it resembles nature. A work is beautiful if it is like nature.[64]

Alain Besançon has suggested that the third critique may be read (albeit discreetly) as an evaluation of Kant's own religious experience. Kant describes aesthetic experience, like that of faith, as being in the presence of the beautiful while being unable to account for it through speech. Though not the same as the mystic's apophatic experience,

---

62. Alexander G. Baumgarten, *Meditationes Philosophicae de Nonnullis Ad Poema Pertinentibus* (1735), as cited in Alejandro Garcia-Rivera, *The Community of the Beautiful*, 9.
63. Hofstadter, *Philosophies*, 278.
64. Ibid., 279.

it is an encounter with "the universal without a concept." Besançon writes: "The beautiful is thus placed within the same perspective as that of God for the believer: a certainty of which one can say nothing, except that it is."[65]

Perhaps it was his desire to understand religious experience that led Kant to his description of the sublime. The sublime is "the absolutely great . . . . It is not permissible to seek for an adequate standard of this outside itself, but merely in itself."[66] He confined the experience of the sublime to encounters with nature. Such encounters are beyond limits, yet intelligible. In a rare poetic moment Kant writes that those who encounter the sublime are "drawn gradually, by the quiet stillness of a summer evening as the shimmering light of the stars breaks through the brown shadows of night and the lonely moon rises into view into high feelings of friendship, of disdain for the world, of eternity."[67] The sublime is identified as a pleasure in the way that nature's capacity to overwhelm our powers of perception and imagination is contained by and fuels our rational comprehension. The sublime engenders "negative pleasure" of admiration, fear, and respect. An encounter with the sublime is a distinctively aesthetic, in some way religious, experience, one that gave Kant occasion to consider his aesthetic theory in greater detail.

Yet the Kantian concept of the sublime points to the greatest obstacle thus far in the history of natural beauty and soteriology. Elaine Scarry has suggested that as the Enlightenment period split the sublime from the beautiful, the extraordinary from the ordinary, which previously had inhabited the same territory in "beauty," the beautiful came under assault. The beautiful became the diminutive,

---

65. Alain Besançon, *The Forbidden Image: An Intellectual History of Iconoclasm*, trans. Jane Marie Todd (Chicago: University of Chicago Press, 2000), 195.
66. Immanuel Kant, *Critique of Judgment*, par. 25, trans J. H. Bernard (New York: Hafner, 1968), 88.
67. As quoted in Besançon, *Forbidden Image*, 198.

and thus dismissible, of the two. Where once there was a path from the meadow flower or mighty tree to what Kant called "eternity," now the path was lined with obstructions. The earlier continuity between the meadow flower and beauty as a transcendental was lost. One no longer could lead to the other. As Scarry puts it, "the sublime now prohibited, or at least interrupted, the easy converse between the diminutive and the distributive."[68] Theologians such as Augustine, Hildegard, and ones even as late as Edwards could not have imagined such a radical impasse in their own experiences of natural beauty in relation to the divine realm.

I have characterized the Enlightenment legacy in aesthetics as the decline of beauty, and theology essentially has been relegated to silence on the subject of beauty through the modern and the beginning of the postmodern period. Tatarkiewicz suggests, however, that modern aesthetics has run its course, and we are on the verge of another turning point in the great theory of beauty. This can be seen in a renewed interest across academic disciplines in the possibility of beauty as a transcendental, or what Scarry calls the "distributive." The modern period brought a kind of hyper-individualism in the world of art. Artists were no longer in relationship to communities, much less religious communities. Abstraction and formalism in art have moved through extremism. And as artists have taken these philosophical streams to their logical conclusions, there seems to be a fresh interest in looking anew at the relationships between artists, human creativity, communities, the beautiful, and beauty. It is precisely this renewed interest that has paved the way for an examination of the art of Andy Goldsworthy in relation to theological aesthetics,[69] asking an ancient question yet one that is newly possible post-Enlightenment, of the relationship

---

68. Elaine Scarry, *On Beauty and Being Just* (Princeton: Princeton University Press, 1999), 85.
69. See chapter three below.

between the experience of natural beauty and insight into the need for human salvation.

Conclusion

People frequently describe their experiences of being on retreat at Camp Mitchell as transformative. The camp is referred to as a place where lives are changed. Using descriptors like "peaceful," "quiet," "beautiful," pilgrims talk about the setting as much as any specific program in which they participated there. It is the beauty of the place that brings people back to the camp year after year. Anecdotally speaking, it is clear that such a natural setting attracts those who are hungry for beauty and opens up the possibility of spiritual renewal. Theologically speaking, it is clear that the camp is a place where aesthetic experience and religious experience meet. And reflection on the experience of the beautiful in central Arkansas is part of an ancient, longstanding tradition that considers such natural beauty in relationship to matters of human redemption. The question is, and has been: how is the experience of the beautiful transformative? How is it redemptive? How are lives changed by beauty?

These questions have been part of Christian theological inquiry since the early church. Influenced by classical aesthetics, in early centuries the church focused on the challenge of achieving a proper vision of beauty, and thus a deeper understanding of the divine, though ultimate fulfillment of that vision would have to wait until life in the resurrection. Natural beauty had the power to reorient the pilgrim in a proper direction, to console the pilgrim on the journey, and to reveal vestiges of a higher, divine beauty. The medieval church tried to grasp beauty in a world that seemed transitory and tragic, though also infused with a beauty continuous with the divine within an integrated order. Natural beauty was a kind of bridge to divine beauty, or at least a starting point on the ascent to God. With the modern period and the rise of scientific methods, philosophical developments, and a tenacious iconoclasm on the religious front, beauty began its decline. Natural beauty was no longer continuous with a higher beauty, as philosophical and religious obstructions emerged. Beauty could distract. It became impossible to obtain access to beauty as a transcendental as the experience of the beautiful was relegated to the subjective realm. Yet even within this decline and amid modern suspicions of beauty, this trajectory of the history of natural beauty in relationship to soteriology generally continued, albeit in quieter ways. Reformers could still find the glory of God in natural beauty and respect the experience of the beautiful as an agent of conversion, secondary to Christ and biblical revelation. Even Immanuel Kant, a champion of the Enlightenment rationalism that tried to relegate the beautiful to a question of taste, was forced to turn uncomfortably to the poetic upon encountering the sublime in nature.

Considering the history of theological reflection on natural beauty, it is clear that over the centuries natural beauty has weathered dramatic shifts in religious and philosophical thought and maintained a place within matters of soteriology. The roles ascribed to that beauty have changed over the centuries, yet the central idea that the experience of natural beauty is redemptive in some way has prevailed. This idea is alive today, and current environmental considerations necessitate an earnest exploration of how such experiences are transformative. How does natural beauty lend insight into the need for human salvation? How might we understand the saving work of beauty, as we struggle to save beauty? To consider these questions, and to explore the nature of the religious insight to be gained from the experience of the beautiful, we turn next to American pragmatist

Josiah Royce and his understanding of where the aesthetic and the religious meet.

2

Nature–Beauty and Salvation

On Earth Day 2011, National Public Radio host Ira Flatow offered a segment called "Listening to Wild Soundscapes" on his show, "Science Friday."[1] Marking the anniversary of the publication of Rachel Carson's book *Silent Spring* as one of the catalysts for the first Earth Day in 1970, he recalled her argument that listening to the sounds of living creatures, or their silence, was a means to understanding the state of the environment.[2] Since then ecologists have turned on their microphones and have been recording all kinds of sounds coming from a variety of landscapes. This exciting new field is called soundscape ecology.

Flatow interviewed bio-acoustician Bernie Krause and Purdue University professor of forestry and natural resources Bryan Pijanowski to understand this new field. His guests described placing digital microphones in landscapes across the globe and capturing a

---

1. Archived at http://www.npr.org/2011/04/22/135634388/listening-to-wild-soundscapes, accessed 7/14/2011.
2. Rachel Carson, *Silent Spring,* 40th Anniversary Ed. (Boston: Mariner Books, 2002).

symphony of sounds made by the inhabitants of those environments. The premise of soundscape ecology is that natural soundscapes are ongoing, profoundly informative narratives that can teach scientists about the relative health or decline of an ecosystem. From a jungle in Madagascar to an underwater recording of a coral reef near Fiji, listeners were treated to samples of such recordings and a cacophony of sounds made by insects, amphibians, mammals, even snapping shrimp and several species of fish. The recordings were described by host Flatow as beautiful and soothing.

Krause discussed his new book, *The Great Animal Orchestra: Finding the Origins of Music in the World's Wild Places*.[3] Collecting such sounds as purring jaguars, snapping shrimp, and cracking glaciers, he explores how soundscapes can help us understand the ways in which wild soundscapes and music are connected. Interestingly, while this field of ecology seeks to capture environments untouched by human sound or development, there is also a fundamental link between such untouched environments and the inspiration for and development of human arts, a connection that is explored similarly by Andy Goldsworthy, as described in chapter three.

The interview took a somber turn when the question of diminishing soundscapes arose. The coral reef sample was contrasted with a recording taken a quarter mile away, where the reef is dying. The soundscape was greatly simplified in sound, with far fewer species represented than in the companion recording from a healthier section of the reef. Krause reported that he has been recording soundscapes since 1968. By the time of the broadcast, in 2011, a full fifty percent of his archive came from habitats that are no longer acoustically viable in a natural state. Half of those soundscapes are

---

3. Bernie Krause, *The Great Animal Orchestra: Finding the Origins of Music in the World's Wild Places* (New York: Little Brown; Hachette Audio, 2012). According to the interview, the original subtitle was "How Animals Taught Us to Dance and Sing."

gone after just over forty years. With soundscape ecology being practiced around the globe now, there is a sense of urgency to record as many natural places as possible in order to preserve sounds that might disappear.[4]

This radio window into the work of soundscape ecology sheds creative light on the overarching theme of this study. In our historical moment of increasing environmental destruction—or disappearing soundscapes—what can be gleaned from the experience of beautiful and soothing soundscapes? Is there a religious dimension to such experiences, a place where the religious meets the aesthetic in the natural world? And if the workings of such a religious dimension were better understood, would we find a more sustainable motivation to preserve those soundscapes?

To investigate these questions I turn to American pragmatist Josiah Royce (1855–1916). I explore his mature philosophy of religion within the context of his larger body of work, examine in detail his understanding of the nature of religious insight, and develop his inkling that natural beauty could be such a source of insight. Finally, I consider his understanding of the Beloved Community as an Ecological Beloved Community, one that experiences natural beauty as a source of religious insight for the whole community.

Josiah Royce:
An Idealist Who Knew Sorrow

Ralph Barton Perry, Josiah Royce's biographer and a student of Royce's friend and rival William James, depicted Royce as essentially sentimental, quaint, outdated, and out of touch as a new century of American philosophy dawned. The horrors of World War I left

<hr>

4. Many of the recordings are available at the Purdue Soundscape Ecology Project website: http://1159sequoia05.fnr.purdue.edu/, accessed 7/14/2011.

little room in the public sphere for the kind of absolute idealism for which Royce was known. Gradually Royce was relegated to the sidelines of the story of American pragmatism and "The Battle of the Absolute," with Charles Sanders Peirce as a predecessor and James as its champion.[5] Recently, however, a resurgence in Roycean scholarship has many scholars writing a different story, one that challenges assumed claims to victory in American pragmatism and insists that Royce's hope for salvation through community is still desperately needed in the even more radically individualistic American society of the twenty-first century.

In an address at the Walton Hotel in Philadelphia in December of 1915, Royce offered his audience an autobiographical sketch of great humility and subtle wit.[6] He provided insights into his intellectual journey, which began in Grass Valley, California in 1855. A born "nonconformist" from a remote gold mining town that was new enough to still be considered a social experiment, he spoke of growing up during the Civil War but having little understanding of its effects far away in the East. His mother, Sarah Royce, was his primary (and formidable) teacher, and though he loved hearing her read Bible stories he was "greatly dissatisfied with the requirements of observance of Sundays, which stand out somewhat prominently in my memory." He learned the art of dialectics from an older sister, and the two proved to be strong-willed and relentless debate partners. Royce had a predilection for applying these skills to preaching to the other boys in town, which, of course, made him exceedingly unpopular. This lack of social success carried over to his San Francisco days, where the country-born Royce attended grammar and high school. He writes: "My comrades very generally found me

5. Bruce Kuklick, *A History of Philosophy in America 1720–2000* (Oxford: Clarendon Press, 2001), 176.
6. From Royce's *The Hope of the Great Community*, in *The Basic Writings of Josiah Royce*, ed. John J. McDermott (Chicago: University of Chicago Press, 1969), 31–38.

disagreeably striking in my appearance, by reason of the fact that I was redheaded, freckled, countrified, quaint, and unable to play boys' games." Royce would later describe his experience of ill treatment by the other boys in *The Problem of Christianity* as what shaped his understanding of original sin.

Royce then traced his academic career, beginning with his first degree from the new University of California. He was influenced in particular by Joseph LeConte, John Stewart Mill, and Herbert Spencer, among others. He studied in Germany next, including an exploration of Romanticism and Kantian philosophy. He then went to Johns Hopkins University, where he met and befriended William James,[7] and then headed back to the University of California for a teaching post. In 1882 he began his east coast teaching career at Harvard University with a one-year appointment during one of James's sabbaticals. Without detailing his pursuits since that time, he ended his autobiographical sketch with the point that his intellectual pursuits had been continually permeated by the theme of community, though clarity on this developed only gradually over time. While he always felt somewhat inept at and slightly rebellious toward being an effective member of a community himself, he came to teach this central point: we are saved through community. He concluded his remarks that evening by turning the attention of the audience away from himself and toward the crisis that faced the Great Community, namely, World War I. Even amid horrors, Royce let himself be led by A. C. Swinburne's poem, *"To hope for a better dawning."*

---

7. Donald Gelpi, *Varieties of Transcendental Experience: A Study in Constructive Postmodernism* (Collegeville, MN: Liturgical Press, 2000), 290.

Key Developments

At first Royce had some difficulty securing a teaching post at Harvard. He started there optimistically in 1882 with a one-year contract at half salary. In 1885 he obtained a permanent position as an assistant professor, and in that same year published *The Religious Aspects of Philosophy*. In that work he developed his insight that, in order for our fallible claims to truth and error to have meaning, there must be a third party: the All-Knower or Absolute Thought, a divine mind that can ultimately arbitrate our conflicting claims to truth and error. John Clendenning suggests that this idea can be seen as an early expression of Royce's more developed triadic theory of interpretation that came to fruition in *The Problem of Christianity*.[8] From that point Royce established himself through lectures, books, and reviews. After slowing down due to a nervous breakdown in 1888 (presumably caused by overwork), he became professor of the History of Philosophy at Harvard in 1892 and served as department chair from 1894–1898.

Royce continued to develop his work in post-Kantian idealism, publishing a series of essays in *Studies in Good and Evil* in 1898. In the introduction to that work he noted that philosophical idealism, if it means anything, denotes a theory of the universe that cannot be divorced from the real-world business of life. "It is not, as many have falsely supposed, a theory of the world founded merely upon *a priori* speculation, and developed solely in the closet. It is, and in its best historical representatives always has been, an effort to interpret the facts of life."[9] Time would show that such defenses of philosophical

---

8. John Clendenning, ed., *The Letters of Josiah Royce* (Chicago: University of Chicago Press, 1970), 24–25.
9. Josiah Royce, *Studies in Good and Evil: A Series of Essays upon Problems of Philosophy and Life* (New York: D. Appleton and Company, 1906), iii–iv.

idealism could not stand up to the devastation of World War I, which must have contributed to Royce's waning popularity in a postwar era.

In 1899–1900, Royce delivered the prestigious Gifford Lectures, which represented a culmination of years of study and were published as *The World and the Individual*. In this two-volume work he sought to offer a general definition of God, the world, the finite individual, and relations among all three. He analyzed the philosophical bases of religious belief and took on the problems of ontology in the first volume through a study of conceptions of being as presented by mysticism, realism, and critical rationalism. Royce offered a fourth conception of being defined in this way: "What is, or what is real, is as such the complete embodiment, in individual form and in final fulfillment, of the internal meaning of finite ideas."[10] He explored this conception in the second volume and gave an account of his theory of knowing the world, human nature, and the moral order. According to Royce in his exploration of the relations between our finite ideas and the ultimate nature of things, the Absolute is the larger Self that includes all finite selves and gives each finite self its ultimate purpose. We seek to know the Absolute (God) to understand our moral destiny. We have moral freedom, and sin is a choice against becoming the self we ought to become. In an idealist perspective on the problem of sin and evil, atonement in the future makes up for present evil. But Royce's was not a facile idealist interpretation of evil in which, from the bird's-eye view of the absolute, everything is fine. As he showed later in *The Problem of Christianity*, evil and human sin have a substantial role in the betterment of the world, but that takes work.[11]

Royce's longtime colleague Charles Sanders Peirce read *The World and the Individual* appreciatively, but strongly urged Royce to study

10. *Letters of Josiah Royce*, 34.
11. Gelpi, *Varieties of Transcendental Experience*, 295–97.

logic. Royce took the challenge and pursued a deeper study of logic and of Peirce's own work. Peirce came to see him as a true pragmatist (or pragmaticist, a term so ugly no one would steal it, as had been the case with "pragmatism," in Peirce's view).[12] Peirce had a significant influence on Royce, as can be seen clearly in his later works. Following the success of his Gifford Lectures, Royce published prolifically and eventually had to scale back again due to health concerns. He decided to concentrate more narrowly on the philosophy of religion.[13]

In 1908 Royce published his major work in ethics, *The Philosophy of Loyalty*, which offered a thoroughgoing critique of American individualism and a resolute emphasis on community. Asking what conditions are necessary for a life to be meaningful, he determined that a morally significant life requires much more than simply doing what we are told is right. One has to act freely, of course, but more importantly, one must act self-consciously. This requires that we commit ourselves to a cause. There are many causes in this world, and we must choose from among them and act in accordance with a deeply held commitment. Examples include a patriot serving his or her country (including, it should be said, a Confederate soldier fighting for the South in the Civil War, thus defending slavery), or a martyr dying for his or her religious convictions; any such commitment should imply at least an openness to the "universal community." This kind of commitment is what Royce called "loyalty." Embracing loyalty, we then join a community of others who are committed to the same cause, developing a morally significant dedication to both the cause and the community. For Royce loyalty is an ideal that makes life meaningful. Loyalty requires real commitment and sacrifice of one's personal interests in service

12. Ibid., 253.
13. Ibid., 292.

of a higher good. Loyalty helps us transcend ourselves. The practice of living loyally bears moral fruit, and loyalty engenders habits that make living in this committed way possible. Loyalty creates and strengthens social ties, so it is good for the individual and for society. This is the antidote to individualism and is what makes life worth living.[14]

Committing to a worthy cause involves discernment since there are so many competing causes in the world. A good cause is one that promotes loyalty in others. An evil cause is one that in effect destroys or impedes truly loyal living. In terms of worthy causes, Royce paid particular attention to loyalty to lost causes, those that cannot be fulfilled or attained by those committed to them, often due to the scope or magnitude of the cause (e.g., attaining all truth or establishing universal loyalty). Rather than giving up on lost causes, one should be loyal to them since they inspire the highest moral commitment.[15] I find this Roycean "lost cause" category of interpretation potentially very fruitful in the overall discussion of the work of environmental justice and restoration.

Royce admitted that there are good causes that are in conflict with each other. This is the tragedy of loyalty, and the question becomes how to choose between good things. Overcoming this tragedy requires loyalty to loyalty and to all loyal persons, taking a kind of bird's eye view of the conflicts. Ultimately, according to Royce, one must be loyal to the system of causes, to that which transcends individual causes. Don Gelpi suggested that here Royce makes a metaphysical move; there is a real unity with all experience, and there is a religious dimension to this unity. Royce has his sights set on the universal community of all the loyal and the universal good

---

14. Kelly A. Parker, "Josiah Royce," *The Stanford Encyclopedia of Philosophy (Continually Updated Resource: Summer 2005 Edition)*, Edward N. Zalta, ed., URL http://plato.stanford.edu/archives/sum2005/entries/royce.

15. Ibid.

of all humanity, which is grounded in real-life, concrete communities of loyalty. The conflicts among good causes ultimately roll up into a more harmonious unity at the level of the universal.[16]

There are important criticisms to be made about Royce's central category of loyalty. He wrote at a time when critique of the United States government was becoming more dangerous. Take, for example, the case of Eugene V. Debs (1855–1926), an American union leader and later Socialist candidate for President. He denounced American participation in World War I in a speech that brought about his arrest in 1918 and his ultimate conviction and imprisonment under the Espionage Act of 1917. Such a political environment is perhaps not very different from American politics in 2014, when critiques of national domestic and foreign policies can be interpreted as unpatriotic, disloyal. Royce, as an idealist, trusted deeply in loyalty to loyalty and the highest aims of human life, but it should be noted that loyalty as a category can be used for less noble purposes than what Royce perhaps imagined.[17]

Royce studied logic throughout his career. He proposed a system of formal logic in 1905 in an essay entitled, "The Relation of the Principles of Logic to the Foundations of Geometry." This developed into his book, *The Principles of Logic*, completed in 1910 and appearing in 1913. Some of Royce's last writings were essays on logic in "Mind," "Negation," and "Order," published in *The Encyclopaedia of Religion and Ethics* in 1916. Kelly Parker suggests that there is much work to be done in exploring Royce's pursuit of mathematics and logic and how that work might clarify and flesh out his ideas in other writings.[18]

16. Gelpi, *Varieties of Transcendental Experience*, 300–3.
17. See Eugene V. Debs, *Debs: His Life, Writings and Speeches* (San Francisco: University Press of the Pacific, 2002).
18. Parker, "Josiah Royce."

In 1912, Royce suffered a stroke, and during his recuperation he began reading Christian theologians and made a more intensive study of the early, middle, and late published works of Charles Peirce, with whose work he was somewhat familiar through years of collaborative study and correspondence. In this new review, Royce had an insight into Peirce's theory of signs and method of interpretation, something that would have a profound influence on his thinking and especially on his masterwork, *The Problem of Christianity*. Royce recounted:

> I often had heard Peirce state, in his own attractive but baffling way, this theory of knowledge. I had supposed it to be fairly well known to me. Yet I had never understood its real force, until I thus saw it in the light of this new review. Then indeed, I observed its close connection with what I had been seeking to formulate in my philosophy of loyalty. I saw also how many aspects of philosophical idealism, when this Peircean theory of knowledge was brought to bear upon them, got a new concreteness, a new significance, and a new relation to the methods and to the presuppositions of inductive science. Thus, by the aid of Peirce, I was led to those considerations about the theory of knowledge which I have tried to set forth in the second volume of my *Problem of Christianity*.[19]

This "Peircean insight" of 1912 helped Royce move from a subject-object or dyadic theory of knowledge to a triadic one, with a sign-sender, a sign-receiver, and a sign-interpreter. He would use this structure to interpret Christianity through a metaphysics of community.[20] Royce also came to take Peirce's concept of "musement" very seriously. Musement is the mind's "Pure Play without any breach of continuity," in which the mind ponders

---

19. Excerpted from Royce's First Berkeley Lecture, 20 July 1914, and reproduced in fuller detail in *Josiah Royce's Late Writings*, vol. 2, ed. Frank M. Oppenheim (Bristol: Thoemmes Press, 2001), 1–19.
20. Frank Oppenheim, *Royce's Mature Philosophy of Religion* (Notre Dame, IN: University of Notre Dame Press, 1987), 23.

freely.[21] Royce employed this method of thinking to muse about the nature of community and Christianity in the last years of his life.

In his few remaining years following this philosophical breakthrough, in addition to *The Sources of Religious Insight* and *The Problem of Christianity*, Royce published *The Hope of the Great Community* in 1916 as well as several articles for the *Encyclopedia of Religion*, final expressions of many of the philosophical themes he developed over decades. For example, in the article "Mind" we find a clear expression of his late theory of metaphysics and epistemology. He discounts approaching the idea of mind from a perceptual or conceptual perspective alone, opting instead for a process of interpretation and signification in community based on his understanding of Peirce. He writes that "a mind is essentially a being that manifests itself through signs" and that, as a reality to be interpreted, mind (when it reaches a relatively full and explicit expression) is "equally definable in terms of two ideas—the idea of the self, and the idea of the community of selves."[22] In his essay on "Negation" we find a mature expression of Royce's understanding of how we come to know what the world ought to be and what we ought to do. By analyzing the "not-relation" we achieve greater clarity of knowledge, as well as a clearer perspective on moral conduct and values. One can see seeds of this theme early in his argument from error, which also seem linked to his understanding of musement later, as he pretends for a moment that one can reach salvation alone without the help of others and without a community altogether. In that line of thought the need for community becomes clear, and thus one can see in these late articles real continuity with

21. Ibid., 9.
22. Josiah Royce, "Mind," 8: 649–57 in *Encyclopaedia of Religion and Ethics*, James Hastings, ed. (New York: Charles Scribner's Sons, 1916).

the theme that pervaded his work: the soteriological nature of community.[23]

Royce continued to lecture and was working on a talk entitled "The Spirit of Community" when World War I broke out. He put that lecture aside and turned his attention to making economic proposals for mediating international conflict, which became *War and Insurance* in 1914.[24] Royce died in September of 1916.

Religious Insight

In 1911, Royce delivered the Bross Lectures in Lake Forest, Illinois; these were published as *The Sources of Religious Insight* the following year. According to the author this book is one of his easiest to read (though deceptively simple with regard to content), and in his own words the book "contains the whole sense of me in a brief compass."[25] Thanks in large part to the success of *The Problem of Christianity,* which came soon after, *Sources* has been often and undeservedly overlooked. In large measure this work was a response to his late friend William James's *Varieties of Religious Experience,* in which, Royce believed, James had overemphasized private religious experience, namely that of the extraordinary variety experienced by extraordinary individuals. Royce was more interested in religious faith as experienced by ordinary people in ordinary communities. He sought to correct James's open-ended pluralism through his insistence on the existence of an actual infinite being.[26] He also moved away from James's use of the unconscious in favor of trying to

---

23. Ibid.
24. Parker, "Josiah Royce."
25. *Letters of Josiah Royce,* 570.
26. Parker, "Josiah Royce."

articulate conscious awareness through religious insight, a particular kind of human understanding available to all.[27]

Royce begins this work with the problem traditionally known as the "salvation of man." The world's major religious traditions share the postulate that humankind needs saving in some way as well as a conviction about the means to attain salvation. Royce explores salvation in general and universal terms; he is not interested in developing these lectures along the lines of Christian dogmatics or that of any other specific religious tradition. He would save an explicitly Christian understanding of atonement for *The Problem of Christianity*. Generally speaking, according to Royce, salvation has something to do with the real meaning of life. The need for salvation stands out among all other human needs as the most crucial. Missing the knowledge of this means missing the highest aim or purpose of one's life altogether. The idea of the need for salvation hinges on two points:

> The first is the idea that there is some end or aim of human life which is more important than all other aims, so that, by comparison with this aim all else is secondary or subsidiary, and perhaps relatively unimportant, or even vain and empty. The other idea is this: That man as he now is, or as he naturally is, is in great danger of so missing this highest aim as to render his whole life a senseless failure by virtue of thus coming short of his true goal.[28]

All depends, Royce concludes, on whether one can gain insight into the nature of this need for salvation. His task is to explore the sources of insight that can yield authentic religious insight into the need and way of salvation.

---

27. Gelpi, *Varieties of Transcendental Experience*, 311.
28. Josiah Royce, *The Sources of Religious Insight* (Washington, DC: Catholic University of America Press, 2001), 12.

Beginning with insight in general, he defines it as "knowledge that makes us aware of the unity of many facts in one whole, and that at the same time brings us into intimate personal contact with these facts and with the whole wherein they are united."[29] There are three marks of an insight: "breadth of range, coherence and unity of view, and closeness of personal touch." Insight is a kind of knowledge from experience that is larger than the experience itself; we come to know more than what we experience. It helps us see unity in variety. And insight makes us personally present to the reality that the insight discloses.

What makes an insight religious in nature? Simply stated, an insight is religious when its object is religious, and a religious insight is essentially redemptive. Religious insight is knowledge of the need and way of salvation. For the one experiencing it, religious insight is ". . . the presence or the coming of the longing for, or the communion with something which [someone] comes to view as the power that may save him from his need, or as the light that may dispel his darkness, or as the truth that shows him the way out, or as the great companion who helps him—in a word, as his Deliverer."[30] With a religious insight, then, one grasps the most important goal of his or her life (and the real and present danger of missing that goal) and comes into some kind of contact with (or receives revelation of) divine aid for the journey. This divine aid is a felt presence that is experienced as savior, liberator, inner strength, illuminator. It is experienced as "working for you," even when there is a felt absence. It is the workings of the invisible church's spirit in our spirits.[31]

There is something paradoxical, however, about the nature of religious experience. How is it that we, who need revelation and

---

29. Ibid., 5–6.
30. Ibid., 28–29.
31. Ibid., 297.

guidance to set us on our path, can tell when we receive such revelation? How will we know when it happens? "The paradox is that a being who is so ignorant of his duty and of his destiny as to need guidance at every point, so weak as to need saving, should still hope, in his fallible experience, to get into touch with anything divine. The question is, how is this possible? What light can my individual experience throw upon vast problems such as this?"[32] Royce determines that for any external revelation to intervene in a person's life, that person's "inner light" or heart must recognize that the revelation is divine. A person's inner light helps him or her see that he or she is in need of deliverance, as well as shedding light on the way of salvation and something of the divine nature that assists us.[33]

It should be noted, however, that there is no easy resolution to this paradox, despite centuries of argumentation.

> Some, including Royce, have tried to throw light on this paradox by using the relation of "nature and supernature" and trying to distinguish this relation as one sometimes of contrariness, sometimes of indiscernibility, and sometimes of levels of our thinking. Few stress the mysteriousness of this relation, even though they teach, not out of philosophy of religion, but out of sacred theology that "grace builds on nature." Yet if that dictum is mainly followed, it leads us to an inability to tell when we are moved by nature as contrasted with when we are moved by grace.[34]

Royce, much like Jonathan Edwards before him, retained a keen sense of the need to discern "spirits." He could not offer a complete resolution to this paradox, and it remained with him throughout his work.

---

32. Ibid., 25.
33. Frank Oppenheim, "Introduction," *Sources of Religious Insight,* xv–xvi.
34. Frank Oppenheim, correspondence with the author, 11/13/2012.

Royce developed seven sources of religious insight. Taken together and integrated, they represent a process of illumination open to all. The seven are personal experience, social experience, reason, will, dedicated loyalty, the religious mission of sorrow, and finally the unity of the Spirit and the invisible church. Royce admits that this is not meant to be an exhaustive list; other sources could include the world of nature, human responses to beauty, the cult of the dead, etc.[35] Though not a complete list of sources, these seven offer an important road map of religious insight, one that ranges from the simplest form of personal and social experience to the most rich and complex form of religious experience mediated through community and the Spirit. The need and way of salvation ultimately draw one redemptively into community.

Royce is trying to show an inherent starting point and path in the spiritual life. He believes that we all feel some kind of burden from which we long to be saved. Each of us has a personal ideal of life, a felt need for salvation, and a longing for contact with that divine power that can save us. We come to know that we cannot achieve salvation alone, which in turn draws us into social experience. The next step is to combine experience with reason to analyze the connections we come to see; this is not abstract reason for reason's sake, but rather reason as a concrete tool for helping us solve the problem of salvation. Our will comes in next, for we then want to get in touch with the bigger picture. These four sources, taken together, guide us to the remaining sources, which are the highest three.

Ethics and duty constitute the fourth source, the religion of loyalty, which calls us to dedicate ourselves to a cause. The cause comes to us as a gift of grace, and it may take many different forms (science, the love of another person, a flag, the church, the cause of humanity,

---

35. Oppenheim, *Royce's Mature Philosophy of Religion,* 98.

God's will, etc.). Despite the variety, there is a unity in which all (good) causes participate. The cause is "some conceived, and yet also real, spiritual unity which links many individual lives in one, and which is therefore essentially superhuman."[36] In dedicating ourselves to a cause, we join the community of other loyalists, and though our causes are different, we are joined together in loyalty on a divine level that transcends the individual.

Royce spent years reflecting on the problem of evil. If evil is not real, then religion seems unnecessary. If it is real, then religion seems doomed to fail.[37] Royce's creative use of this dilemma is to suggest carefully that evil or the experience of ill may be "productive" if such suffering is translated into sorrow. The religious mission of sorrow is the sixth source of insight. Sorrow, Royce believed, was not a barrier to religious life but a font of wisdom, a kind of window through which we come to see new possibilities and wider perspectives of the spiritual realm. This view then inspires one to loyal and atoning service.[38]

> In other words, the ills that we *can* spiritualise and idealise without merely destroying them hint to us that, despite the uncomprehended chaos of seemingly hopeless tragedy with which for our present view human life seems to be beset, the vision of the spiritual triumph of the good which reason and loyalty present to us need not be an illusion, but is perfectly consistent with the facts. . . . We have sources of insight which tend to our salvation by showing us . . . the nature of the spiritual process which, as these sources of insight persistently point out, constitutes the essence of reality.[39]

Royce was no stranger to sorrow, especially after the deaths of his adult first-born son and of his friend William James. For him, sorrow

---

36. *Sources of Religious Insight*, 199.
37. Ibid., 226.
38. Oppenheim, "Introduction," *Sources of Religious Insight*, xviii.
39. *Sources of Religious Insight*, 237.

in human life yields insight into reality and inspires loyal living. Again Royce finds a uniting force in this source, with a deep optimism that evil and suffering will grant us a vision of the triumph of the good and thus affirm our path of loyalty and reason as the road that leads to that vision.

The final source on this journey is the unity of the spirit and the invisible church. Some would argue that Christian churches are the highest source of insight into the way and need of salvation. Royce argues from a strong ecumenism that all true loyalists and communities of the loyal (all of which are actually religious in nature) are connected in what he calls the invisible church.

> I call the community of all who have sought salvation through loyalty the Invisible Church . . . . I say that whatever any form of the visible church has done or will do for the religious life of mankind, the crowning source of religious insight is, for us all, the actual loyalty, service, devotion, suffering, accomplishment, traditions, example, teaching, and triumphs of the invisible church of all the faithful.[40]

The pinnacle of the sources, then, is a kind of enlightenment about life lived in the unity of the Spirit. All people dedicated to genuine loyalty are connected to the invisible church. This is important since no individual community has the whole picture; just as individuals need salvation, so do communities themselves, regardless of religious denomination. Only the divine mind can reconcile all of our conflicting viewpoints.[41] The significance of this idea is that no individual and no earthly, finite community achieves salvation alone. We can only grasp ultimate meaning through the experience of communion with all of the communities of loyalty.

Royce's term "sources" seems to have different meanings. On the one hand, it refers to ways in which we are almost hard-wired to

---

40. Ibid., 280.
41. Gelpi, *Varieties of Transcendental Experience*, 313–14.

embark on a spiritual journey toward salvation. These are insights we have on our own and those we gain through social experience, suffering, and loyalty to our cause. They are those elements in the spiritual life that Royce believes have universal recognition. On the other hand, "sources" seems also to refer to a triadic theory of interpretation between individuals, the great community or universal church, and the divine Spirit. While his list of seven ingredients of the spiritual life seems simple at first glance, the journey he describes, which culminates in ultimate meaning, universal community, and the actual possibility of both revelation and salvation, is nothing short of profound.

A final note about Royce's reflective method. In order to test the genuineness of a source he reflects on its contradiction. For example, for the second source he might try to imagine *not* needing anyone else's help on the way to salvation. Since he knows that to be false in his heart of hearts, he concludes that one must need social experiences and community along the way.[42] As mentioned above, he names beauty as a source of religious insight in a letter but does not develop it in the context and seemingly linear trajectory of *The Sources of Religious Insight*. One wonders just where Royce would place beauty in the schema. Is beauty that which can draw us beyond ourselves, into community, and if so, how? Is beauty a cause that inspires genuine loyalty, say through creating or supporting fine art, or perhaps preserving natural beauty? Does beauty offer us a glimpse of spiritual truth of the same scope and magnitude that suffering can offer about the nature of human and divine life? Can beauty be a mechanism for overcoming sectarianism and promoting genuine community? Drawing upon his reflective method, these questions seem equally insightful when approached through negation, such as

---

42. Oppenheim, "Introduction," xix.

whether we even need beauty in our lives. The answer is instinctively obvious, and Royce's complex understanding of the nature of religious insight offers a productive set of tools for exploring how the experience of beauty might yield insight into the way of and the need for salvation.

The Problem of Christianity, the Problem of Evil, and the Beloved Community

While in *The Sources of Religious Insight* Royce tackled religious experience generally, he turned next to Christianity in his masterwork, *The Problem of Christianity,* and asked the fundamental question: "In what sense, if any, can the modern man consistently be, in creed, a Christian?"[43] Looking for a way to justify Christian belief and practice in the modern world without appealing to ideas like mysticism, dogma, or pietism, Royce reframed Christianity as a religion of loyalty (with loyalty as "the *practically devoted love of an individual for a community*"[44]), whose central idea is the Beloved Community and its redeeming function for relieving the moral burden we all sense.[45]

> If indeed I myself must cry "out of the depths" before the light can come to me, it must be my Community that, in the end, saves me. To assert this and to live this doctrine constitute the very core of Christian experience, and of the "Religion of Loyalty." In discussing "the varieties of religious experience," which here concern us, I have everywhere kept this thesis in mind.[46]

43. Josiah Royce, *The Problem of Christianity*, vol. 1, *The Christian Doctrine of Life*; vol. 2, *The Real World and the Christian Ideas*, with a Foreword by Frank M. Oppenheim, S.J. (Washington, DC: Catholic University of America Press, 2001; orig. publication New York: Macmillan, 1913), 62. There are several reformulations of the "problem" throughout the work.
44. Ibid., 41.
45. "Author's Preface," *The Problem of Christianity*, 41. Emphasis in original.
46. Ibid.

Royce is not concerned with individual experiences here, as in James's *Varieties*, but rather with social forms of religious experience. He does not attempt a Christology in this work. His focus is on the community of believers: "the Church, rather than the person of the founder, ought to be viewed as the central idea of Christianity."[47] He turns to early Pauline communities as the best examples we have of graced community. In the early church he finds believers who were bound together by loyalty and guided by the divine Interpreter Spirit, and who strove together toward the Beloved Community through a process of interpretation. In the first volume of *The Problem of Christianity*, Royce develops the "Christian Doctrine of Life," followed in the second volume[48] by the metaphysical implications of that doctrine. It is important to note that in this study Royce takes the perspective of a friendly philosophical critic rather than that of an apologist or hostile critic. In a sense he is sympathetic to both ends of that spectrum and finds it useful to be in a dialectical position between the two extremes.[49]

In the first volume Royce, who was thoroughly versed in the New Testament, reflects on Jesus' preaching about the kingdom of heaven and salvation through membership in that spiritual community and then chooses three essential ideas on which to focus. These are the church or Beloved Community, the moral burden of the individual (sin), and atonement. He turns to Paul's writings about the early Christian communities in order to explore these ideas, since Royce believed that Jesus' sayings alone were insufficient; those teachings needed to be augmented by the experiences of the early communities that tried to live them out after his death and resurrection. In terms of community, Royce found individuals living loyally, transformed

47. Ibid., 43.
48. Josiah Royce, *The Problem of Christianity*, vol. 2: *The Real World and the Christian Ideas*.
49. Smith, "Introduction," *The Problem of Christianity*, 6.

by their loving service into the larger body of Christ. In terms of sin, Royce posited that, given the workings of human nature within the social character of human life, conflict in community is inevitable, and in community we become conscious of the real possibility of social and moral betrayal.[50] This leads him to his creative understanding of atonement.

Early Pauline communities were committed to the idea that salvation only comes (in Royce's language) through faithful loyalty to the beloved religious community. This also requires loyalty of the particular community to a higher realm of grace, to the universal community. So there are two levels of consciousness, the individual and the communal.[51] Sin, then, is disloyalty to those ideals that bind the community together. Sin is about betraying your community (or about a community going astray from the divine Spirit). Royce calls this treason, an act that is historically irrevocable (thus having profound psychological weight for the traitor) but that yields interesting fruit when the sinner is forgiven. Upon forgiveness, which is a deep expression of loyalty sustained in the face of betrayal, the traitor is restored to the community that was betrayed. Forgiveness thus transforms the treachery, and the world is a better place than before this opportunity for loyalty to shine. We have many accounts of Pauline Christians experiencing this kind of healing through the atoning love of the community. That love, or forgiveness, is greater than any treason that temporarily shattered the community. While many find such arguments for the "usefulness" of sin unsettling, Royce's understanding of the power of atoning love has enormous pastoral implications for individuals and communities alike. To Royce's credit as well, the language of treason and

---

50. Gelpi, *Varieties of Transcendental Experience*, 321.
51. Oppenheim, "Foreword," *The Problem of Christianity,* xxv.

restoration within the philosophy of loyalty is a creative naming of a perennial aspect of the human condition.

In *The Christian Doctrine of Life*, then, Royce has explained why Christianity is relevant to modern people. The experience of the Pauline communities names something universal about human life and offers us a model that insists on lived experience in a community for the possibility of atonement. This loyal participation in community is both what saves us and what gives our lives their ultimate meaning.[52] Royce has thus far applied his philosophy of loyalty to Christianity and to the interpretation of the Pauline understanding of love within the context of the Beloved Community. In the second volume he turns to the metaphysical implications of these ideas.

In *The Real World and the Christian Ideas*, Royce sets himself the task of using Peirce's semiotics and theory of interpretation to define the nature of community and apply this to the Beloved Community. He asserts that the universe is a community of interpretation, full of signs that need interpretation. Fundamental to this process is the understanding that interpretation involves three terms, not two: "Thus an interpretation is a relation which not only involves three terms, but brings them into a determinate order. One of the three terms is the interpreter; a second term is the object—the person or the meaning or the text—which is interpreted; the third is the person to whom the interpretation is addressed."[53] Since in a universe of signs every interpretation requires further interpretation in this triadic social structure of knowledge, the process of interpretation is ongoing.

This triadic process, which rejects the idea that an individual can come to knowledge through perception or conception alone, has the

---

52. Gelpi, *Varieties of Transcendental Experience*, 325.
53. *The Problem of Christianity*, 287.

power to mediate conflicts of opinion or belief in a community of interpreters if they are all committed to loyally reaching further for the truth (though understanding reality in the larger picture will only come to fruition in the unforeseeable future). This requires the "will to interpret," in which the search for common meaning transcends temporary conflicts of interpretation. The will to interpret is the embodiment of the will to community in the religion of loyalty. Just as we cannot be saved on our own, we cannot find truth alone. As Don Gelpi summarizes: "Authentic loyalty to a community, of necessity then, incorporates the will to interpret, and the will to interpret seeks to create the shared consensus which mediates shared communal awareness."[54]

Moving beyond individual communities, Royce extends the will to interpret to the world (or universe, reality, etc.).

> Our Doctrine of Signs extends to the whole world the same fundamental principle. The World is the Community. The world contains its own interpreter. Its processes are infinite in their temporal varieties. But their interpreter, the spirit of this universal community,—never absorbing varieties or permitting them to blend,—compares and, through a real life, interprets them all.[55]

It is interesting to note that, as Frank Oppenheim points out, as his philosophy of interpretation developed, Royce moved away from his earlier language of the "Absolute" to "Interpreter-Spirit" as a controlling image of the divine.[56] Interpretation is something of a graced search for meaning, in which the ongoing process of interpretation is infused with the Spirit of the universal community.

There is an important temporal aspect to interpretation. Using the example of a human self, Royce says that we each look to our past

---

54. Gelpi, *Varieties of Transcendental Experience*, 332.
55. *The Problem of Christianity*, 362.
56. Oppenheim, "Foreword," *The Problem of Christianity*, xxix.

and our future to understand who we are, and that who we were in the past, who we are now, and who we will be form a triadic unity of the self (to be interpreted in real life, in social situations). Similarly, the Beloved Community has a past, present, and future that need interpretation. It remembers the ministry, teachings, death, and resurrection of Jesus and looks to the future, anticipating the coming of the kingdom of heaven (or universal community), which is the community's cause. Avoiding much in the way of doctrine or dogma, Royce determines that the Beloved Community is thus a community of memory and hope.

It seems that by "Christian," Royce meant a genuine loyalist dedicated to the cause of the Beloved Community. Being a Christian on Royce's terms means living out one's spiritual and moral journey rooted in an actual community, one that has the Beloved Community (i.e., the kingdom of God or a community of all genuine loyalists) as its cause. It means coming to know oneself, fellow travelers, and the divine in an ongoing process of triadic interpretation that involves the past, present, and future. It means living out atoning love and restoring one another through forgiveness when we stumble. It means being able to move beyond the paralyzing moral burden of each individual in order to find the ultimate meaning of our lives. Don Gelpi suggests that with this religion of loyalty Royce was actually doing Peircean aesthetics (in which the ideals that engage the human conscience must first capture and claim the human heart), though Royce never developed a normative aesthetics.[57] I will explore this further in the section on beauty below.

---

57. Gelpi, *Varieties of Transcendental Experience*, 335.

Notes on the Problem of Evil

Royce struggled with the problem of evil for decades while other philosophers left it alone as a more properly theological problem. As Frank Oppenheim suggests, Royce, as an idealist, believed in the teleological nature of the universe, which made the existence of evil a philosophical question that could not be avoided.[58] And he himself was not a stranger to suffering. George Herbert Palmer once wrote of Royce that "to his happy home came many sorrows, 'afflictions sorted, anguish of all sizes.'"[59] One can get a glimpse of this in reading about the religious mission of sorrow in *The Sources of Religious Insight*, in which Royce struggles to find a way to work through the experience of sorrow to something greater without glossing over the often inscrutable quality of our suffering. He was intent on avoiding a kind of naïve idealism that ultimately argues of the problem of evil that somehow, as John McDermott summarized, "it's all for the best."[60]

In a discussion of Royce's treatment of evil in *The Problem of Christianity,* Oppenheim asks whether his theory of atonement was too neat and artificial, a bit too Hegelian in how the traitor's deed is countered by the atoner's deed and then all is taken up into the community's spirit of loyalty.[61] Fortunately, Royce continued to develop his response to the problem of evil in the remaining years of his life, benefiting from years of consideration before his later formulations. We see more humility in the last of his writings on the problem than in his earlier periods. He came to rely less on

58. Frank Oppenheim, *Reverence for the Relations of Life: Re-imagining Pragmatism via Josiah Royce's Interactions with Peirce, James, and Dewey* (Notre Dame, IN: University of Notre Dame Press, 2005), 416–17.
59. George Herbert Palmer, "Dedication," in *Contemporary Idealism in America*, ed. Clifford Barrett (New York: The Macmillan Company, 1932), 9.
60. John J. McDermott, "Moral and Religious Experience," *The Basic Writings of Josiah Royce*, 829.
61. Oppenheim, *Reverence*, 411–12.

philosophy's promise of solving a riddle and more on the divine guidance of the Interpreter (or "Logos-Spirit" in late writings) in the healing/reconciling aspect of the process of interpretation. He advocated an "unearthly confidence and hope" that it would all work out in the end for those who live dutifully. This stance requires courage and trust in the wisdom and grace of the Interpreter Spirit of the Universal Community.[62] Highlighting this aspect of human limitation and the need for hope in the religion of loyalty allows for a more humanly fitting soteriology that can hold the good and ill together with all of the realism and optimism Royce can muster.

Hope for the Beloved Community

As we have seen, Royce's philosophy of loyalty offers a profound challenge to American ethics rooted in the national virtue of individualism. He believed that in order to live a moral life one must choose a cause, devote oneself to that cause, and serve it in the spirit of loyalty itself. Further, without membership in community with other loyalists we run the risk of never discovering the very meaning of our lives. Without community we cannot fully know ourselves, the world we live in, or the Divine. In *The Hope of the Great Community*, Royce looked at the fragmentation of that great community in a time of war and offered a "Song before Sunrise."[63] He characterized the conflict of World War I as one between the community of humankind and the particular interests of individual nations. It was not the victory or defeat of particular nations that was at stake. Rather, Royce believed that the cause of humanity in its wholeness (or the church universal) was on the line.[64] In his optimism about

---

62. Ibid., 418–19.
63. Josiah Royce, *The Hope of the Great Community* (New York: Macmillan, 1916), 26.
64. Ibid., 31–33.

the future triumph of the great community he writes of a sense of hope on the other side of the present conflict: "Every idealist believes himself to have rational grounds for the faith that somewhere, and in some world, and at some time, the ideal will triumph, so that a survey, a divine synopsis of all time, somehow reveals the lesson of all sorrow, the meaning of all tragedy, the triumph of the spirit."[65]

Despite, or perhaps because of the current circumstance, Royce held his ground that salvation will come through the willing service of a community, not to a detached individual. ". . . the salvation of the world will be found, if at all, through uniting the already existing communities of mankind into higher communities . . . ."[66] In that future unity, though distinctions will be maintained, there will be a common spirit like that which comes from loyalty to a kind of Pauline charity.

Royce turned his attention to the practical work of finding a solution to the present fragmentation of competing nationalisms. He believed that insurance would be the key for international unification, based on a triadic model of the adventurer, the beneficiary (these first two having conflicting interests), and the insurer or reconciler. These three would become a community of interpretation that could mediate between national interests and find a higher peace. He spelled this out in *War and Insurance*,[67] and believed that this triadic process of interpretation was the way to peace.

If World War I was a watershed for (at least the public perception of) Royce's absolute idealism, how much greater is the challenge of

---

65. Ibid., 27.
66. Ibid., 49.
67. Josiah Royce, *War and Insurance: An Address Delivered Before the Philosophical Union of the University of California at its Twenty-Fifth Anniversary at Berkeley, California, August 27, 1914* (New York: Macmillan: 1914).

giving Royce a fair hearing today. At the outbreak of the Great War, Royce saw the destruction born of individualism and disloyalty, and he continued to teach loyalty and say that salvation is possible. In a world marred by wars, globalization, cycles of poverty and violence, terrorism, epidemics, and the uncertainties of climate change, I wonder whether Royce would maintain his optimism about a kind of universal human nature and ultimate unity in the future. Would he have hope? There is no way to know, of course, though it is likely that his thoroughgoing commitment to the Beloved Community as a community of memory and hope and his belief in its power to save us would not be deterred. The terms of public debate and moral discourse seem more complex, given the global events and emergent voices since his death. Yet his realism about human conflict and the problems of evil and suffering make him "one of us" in today's world rather than a dismissible quaint philosopher. I think of the dedicated loyalty of Martin Luther King, Jr., who studied Royce and who serves as a reminder that Royce's philosophy can be a powerful instrument in today's causes. The challenge is to learn his ideas deeply enough to teach them and preach them in the languages of our time. I am convinced after these encounters with Royce that his ideas can help us better understand the world we live in, find inspiration for our causes, and sustain hope for the great community.

Sketches of Beauty and Royce's Hidden Aesthetics

Charles Peirce mapped the Good, the True, and the Beautiful to ethics, logic, and aesthetics. These, he believed, are normative sciences for "right thinking"; that is, we know how we ought to act (ethics) only by engaging rationality (logic) to discern ideals (aesthetics). For Peirce what truly captures the human heart is discerning proper aims or ideals, which appear to us as "beautiful." So, following this argument, it is clear that Royce's philosophy of loyalty is his aesthetics.

Yet there is important exploration to be done of what Alejandro García-Rivera calls Royce's "hidden aesthetics."[68] Though he shied away from aesthetics formally, Royce offered several clues to how beauty functions. As seen in the following four brief sketches, beauty is a source of religious insight, a needed element of training in loyalty, a means through which we come closer to the divine, and a cousin of the good. Following these sketches is an attempt to chart natural beauty as a source of religious insight.

To begin, let us return to Royce's reflections on his childhood as he led his December 1915 audience to the time when he delighted in sunsets, deeply impressed by the "wide prospects when one looked across the wide Sacramento Valley."[69] Once in San Francisco, this boy was at first only "fascinated" by the Pacific Ocean, but as a mature adult he was "taught" more than a little by the oceans.[70] Through his hiking in the hills around Grass Valley and later in the Oakland hills and still later in Yosemite with his son Stephen, this "woodsman" breathed in what he called the *vis medicatrix naturae* (nature's healing power). It is clear from these instances that Royce himself was saved by beauty.[71]

1. Childlike Wonder

In a letter to his friend Richard Cabot in June 1912, Royce agreed that beauty should have been included in the list of sources of religious insight. "Personally, I have *some* access to beauty especially

---

68. Alejandro García-Rivera, *The Community of the Beautiful: A Theological Aesthetics* (Collegeville, MN: Liturgical Press, 1999), 143–46.
69. *Hope of the Great Community*, 123.
70. Ibid., 126.
71. Frank Oppenheim, correspondence with the author, 11/13/2012.

in *two* realms, viz.; music, and nature-beauty; together with a fairly warm, but, as you know, limited access to poetry. As to music and nature-beauty, I am, and must remain, naïve, ignorant,—at best childlike." He speaks of his childhood in California and lack of cultivation in such things as art appreciation, perhaps leaving him with a sense of limitation as he tried to find adequate language for the experience of beauty. "Of beauty, therefore, I must not prophesy. The less I say about beauty, the more sincere will be, and sound, the little that I have any right on occasion to stammer. . . . So when I get my moment or days of enjoyment of beauty,—alone with the sea, or with the hills,—or when my soul gets free again to listen a little to . . . music,—well, when such times come to me, I try to remain a little child as to beauty, and to say nothing."[72]

It is clear that Royce finds experiences of beauty in nature and music to be illuminating, though he hesitates to put language to those experiences for fear of missing the mark of what they mean to him. However, we can assume that if beauty is, in fact, a source of religious insight, as he suggests, the experience of beauty yields insight into the need and way of salvation.

2. Training in Loyalty

In *The Philosophy of Loyalty*, Royce teaches that experiences of beauty are needed for training in loyalty:

> Art supports loyalty whenever it associates our cause with beautiful objects, whenever it sets before us the symbols of our cause in any worthy expression, and whenever, again, by showing us any form of the beautiful, it portrays to us that very sort of learning and unity that loyalty ceaselessly endeavors to bring into human life. Thus viewed, art may be a teacher of loyalty. . . . I am attempting here no theory of

---

72. *Letters of Josiah Royce*, 577–78.

art. But it belongs to our present province merely to insist that part of our education in loyalty is to be won through whatever love of beauty and whatever knowledge of the beautiful we possess. . . . Whatever is beautiful appears to us to embody harmonious relations. And the practical search for harmony of life constitutes loyalty. And thus training for loyalty includes the knowledge of the beautiful.[73]

Art and the beautiful here are among the teachers of loyalty, for they appear to us as the embodiment of harmonious relations, which in turn help us to see that unity for which loyalty strives in the great community of all the loyal.

3. The Fulfillment of The Mystical

In *Metaphysics* we find Royce sharing his experience of listening to Bach, particularly his "St. Matthew's Passion."

When the understanding of life takes the form of a process, a process every stage of which has been already attained, a process guided by the chronosynoptic vision of the whole, then you are dealing with that which is beyond mysticism and that which is at the same time the fulfillment of mysticism, the union of satiety and activity, of triumph and peace in triumph, the kind of union which Paul depicts in 1 Cor. XIII: "For now we see through a glass, darkly; but then face to face. Now I know in part; but then shall I know even as also I am known."[74]

Having already learned that the beauty of music is a source of insight, here Royce explores the way in which music guides us toward union with God, seeing face to face. The experience of listening to "St. Matthew's Passion," for example, enables one to see interpretation as a process in time and, taken as a whole, that which brings one in a profoundly satisfying way to the fulfillment of mysticism.

73. Josiah Royce, *The Philosophy of Loyalty* (New York: Macmillan, 1908), 289–90.
74. Josiah Royce, *Metaphysics* [1915–16], William Ernest Hocking, Richard Hocking, and Frank M. Oppenheim, eds. (Albany, NY: State University of New York Press, 1998), 211.

4. Beauty as a Pleasurable Good

As part of his 1915–16 extension course in ethics at Boston University, Royce addressed beauty in his lecture, "Pleasure and Pain; Happiness and Unhappiness."

> Plainly, the beautiful is, to any one who enjoys it, a good. But it is a good that we get in consequence of so many conditions, some of them due to our sensations, others to what Wallas calls the pattern to which the objects of our sense-experience conform, that this instance, taken in itself, furnishes an ideally useful example of the distinction between what one might call the direct, or the raw pleasures and pains of our senses, and the wonderful wealth of the world of our feelings. Beauty, in so far as it is presented to our senses, gives us joy by its pleasantness. Its opposite, the ugly, repels us by its disagreeable character. But how hard it is here to formulate how the facts of sense are related to the feelings that the beautiful and the ugly arouse in us.[75]

Here we see Royce hesitating again about an explicit theory of aesthetics and the relationship between sensory input and knowledge in particular. He raises the question of the continuity between senses and feelings, though that question remains unresolved. What this excerpt does show is Royce's lasting concern with both the good (related to the beautiful) and the ugly. A Roycean understanding of beauty as a source of insight must also take the ugly (or evil, sin, etc.) into account as part of an honest (i.e., practical) aesthetic theory.

In his letter to Cabot, Royce writes: "What beauty I *have* known has meant to me some things that I long to be able to say, if so I might, and that have brightened the world for me with a light that I deeply wish to be able to characterize."[76] In these four sketches we see glimpses of what Royce longed to say. Beauty is *at least* a source of religious insight, a teacher of loyalty, a revealer of the divine, and

---

75. Josiah Royce, "Pleasure and Pain; Happiness and Unhappiness," from his 1915–1916 extension course in ethics at Boston University. In Oppenheim, ed., *Josiah Royce's Late Writings*, 106–16.
76. *Letters of Josiah Royce*, 578.

a cousin of the good. These glimpses of an aesthetic theory reveal a rich resource within Royce's mature philosophy.

Natural Beauty as a Source of Religious Insight

These Roycean sketches of beauty suggest that we need to experience it. This seems obvious, but why is this so? Anecdotally, we might say that the experience of the beautiful offers many elements of a richly lived and examined life. The arts, for example, can offer inspiration, wonder about human creativity, education, and a clearer sense of the truth of their subjects and, simultaneously, of ourselves. Natural beauty can offer such things as solace or escape from the stresses of life; it can give a sense of blessedness or abundance and insights beyond ourselves; and it can inspire a sense of wonder about the divine.

Using Royce's own process of negation, when we posit a life *without* beauty we consider the prospect of a radically diminished life. Take, for example, a child in a dense urban area who never experiences green or wild spaces. Imagine a child who is not exposed to museums or cultural events. Surely these are real scenarios for far too many. And so we ask, what is the dilemma of a life without natural beauty or the arts? There seems to be an obvious diminishment. We would assume that such a life comes with greater challenges for striving for one's highest aim or finding ultimate meaning. And if we use Royce's language about insight into the need and way of salvation, a life without beauty is one that might miss this insight. So now, with the intuition that we all need beauty, argued both from common experiences and from negation, I turn to a consideration of natural beauty as a source of religious insight. This theme will be developed more fully in relation to ecological theology, in the proposal of a theological aesthetics of nature in the fourth chapter. For now let us return to Kathleen Moore's experience of the sublime in a thunderstorm as the example of natural beauty for consideration.

Moore describes how she was attracted to storms as a child because there was something beautiful about them and they offered that "blow-to-the-gut awareness of chaotic forces unleashed and uncontrolled, the terror—and finally the awe. . . ."[77] To analyze this experience using Royce's language of insight, first we must note that this is not an extraordinary mystical experience had by an extraordinary individual but rather an experience of beauty in the natural world that is relatively common and open to all. Her experience gave her a sudden insight that there is "power and possibility in the universe greater than anyone can imagine." According to her description, this experience carried the three marks of insight in general: breadth of range, coherence or unity of view of something larger, and closeness of personal touch (that "blow-to-the-gut awareness"). Now the question becomes: is this experience inherently religious? How can natural beauty be a source of religious insight, not just insight in general?

The key, I believe, is Moore's language about craving such experiences of the beautiful. Royce argued that we all have a felt need for salvation and a longing for contact with the divine power than can save us. That, coupled with the ever-present danger of missing the highest aims in life or the real meaning of our journeys, gives us a desire for experiences that expand our understanding and lead us to our salvation. When we have such an experience we have come into contact with a source of religious insight, and the experience is fundamentally redemptive. This is what Moore craved—and, I would argue, received—in those thunderstorms.

77. See the Introduction, p. 2.

It should be noted that christological considerations about human salvation are beyond the scope of this project. I am exploring what happens when the religious and the aesthetic meet, and what kind of insight is gained in the experience of natural beauty. We can take such an experience of natural beauty and map it according to the seven sources explicitly developed by Royce as a process of illumination, adding his pieces of a fledgling aesthetic theory as well. To begin this mapping, we observe that the experience of a beautiful storm begins as a personal sense of longing or craving and answers a felt need for salvation from a power greater than ourselves. We experience childlike wonder when this craving is satisfied and the presence or handiwork of such a power is revealed. We can even achieve what Royce described as the fulfillment of the mystical (or Kant's sublime) in a thunderstorm. This initial stage also captures Royce's view of beauty as a pleasurable good (perhaps with echoes of Thomas Aquinas). There is joy in the experience of natural beauty, a beauty that we understand as inherently good.

In the process of illumination, following the individual experience, we then realize that we cannot achieve salvation on our own; at the same time we long to share such experiences of wonder in the natural world, so we turn to social experience. We are drawn into community. We then try to analyze the connections we come to see through our reason. The will comes next, for we then want to get in touch with the bigger picture and strive for higher aims in life.

Dedicated loyalty follows next, and Royce claimed that beauty can help train us in loyalty. If natural beauty leads us to a particular cause to which we ought to be loyal, it is ecological redemption. If we come to understand that natural beauty is a source of religious insight we need to preserve and tend to that beauty so that it is available to the greater community of interpreters, now and in the future. With natural beauty as a source of religious insight we are led to dedicated loyalty to ecological redemption, a cause that is perhaps among the highest aims of human life in an ecological age and is fundamentally connected to concerns for social justice.

This cause helps us to see the connections between humanity's need for salvation and ecological redemption. Perhaps, as we experience natural beauty, we gain insight into the ways our patterns of living and consumption are unsustainable (symbolic, perhaps, of humanity in a fallen state) and commit ourselves to the cause of ecological health and well-being. We come to see that unexamined and destructive ways of life actually destroy one of the sources of religious insight that has the power to help us see beyond ourselves and behold our need for salvation from outside ourselves. Living in loyalty to the cause of sustainability, on the other hand, gives us the chance to live for higher and less selfish aims than, say, the unexamined accumulation of consumer goods.

There is also a role for the religious mission of sorrow in this process of illumination. Those wonderful, expansive experiences of beauty in nature can lead to a profound sense of how much of created beauty has already been lost or destroyed. Sallie McFague talks about the role of despair in ecological work;[78] grief over environmental destruction, the loss of soundscapes, cannot be avoided, and it can actually help fuel good work. For many, it is too overwhelming to look at the state of the natural world, a point well made by Al Gore in the 2006 documentary on climate change, "An Inconvenient Truth."[79] What happens when we turn away from such difficult truths supports Royce's contention that we are ever in danger of missing our need for salvation and the highest aim of our lives.

In this section I have attempted to develop Royce's claim that natural beauty should be included among the sources of religious

78. Lectures by Sallie McFague at Episcopal Divinity School, Fall 2007.
79. "An Inconvenient Truth," Lawrence Bender Productions, 2006.

insight. Living through a thunderstorm is an experience of the sublime, a power beyond us that helps us to understand our own need for salvation. This is different from private mystical experience; Royce teaches us that, along with other sources of religious insight, such an experience of natural beauty can draw us into a community of others dedicated to loyalty, a community committed to ecological restoration and well-being. In that process we glimpse our own need for salvation and learn to live our lives for higher aims and thus find their meaning. The final fulfillment of this process of illumination was Royce's Beloved Community, a community of memory and hope, ever interpreting meaning into the future. Such a community can be re-imagined in light of what natural beauty has to teach.

The Ecological Beloved Community

The project of appropriating Royce's philosophy of religion and aesthetics for ecological theology can benefit greatly from his understanding of the invisible church, or Beloved Community. He saw it as a community of interpreters engaged in what Gelpi calls a graced search for meaning, guided by the divine Interpreter-Spirit and made beloved by the Deliverer. It is a community with a past, a present, and a future, all of which need interpretation. In Christian terms, the community remembers the ministry, teachings, death, and resurrection of Jesus and looks to the future, anticipating the coming of the kingdom of heaven (or universal community). It is a community of memory and hope.

In light of the environmental crisis, perhaps the Beloved Community needs to be expanded to include more members. As early as 1949, conservationist and naturalist Aldo Leopold advocated for a new sense of community. He suggested a land ethic that would enlarge the boundaries of the community of consideration to include soils, waters, plants, and animals. For Leopold the land was a community that included all things on, over, or in the earth. Harmony with land, he suggested, is like harmony with a friend; you cannot cherish his right hand and chop off his left. The land is one organism.[80]

One can see this early environmental insight developed more fully in the partnership ethic of University of California professor Carolyn Merchant. This environmental ethic assumes that the greatest good for the human and nonhuman communities lies in their mutual interdependence and that the different communities are engaged in a dialectical process of interpretation. Given the global ecological crisis (climate change, ozone depletion, deforestation, soil erosion, population growth, loss of biodiversity, etc.), a new consciousness is needed in which human and nonhuman communities are considered morally and an ecologically sound management that has the health of both in mind is created. A partnership ethic uses the model of a council of all beings in which human and nonhuman members are at the discussion table and there is equity among the conversation partners.[81] This is a fitting image for a Beloved Community of interpreters in an ecological age. It is much like those soundscapes described in the radio interview at the beginning of this chapter. The soundscape of an ecological beloved community would include the mixture of sounds from the natural ecosystems and human communities. A graced search for meaning that is truly hopeful can no longer be limited to human considerations, but must listen to the entire soundscape.

At the suggestion of Frank Oppenheim, I add that this project invites us to understand our earth as a truly beloved one. The

---

80. Aldo Leopold, *A Sand County Almanac* (New York: Ballantine Books, 1949), 189–90.
81. Lecture by Carolyn Merchant, University of California at Berkeley, 5/12/2003. See Carolyn Merchant, *Earthcare: Women and the Environment* (New York: Routledge, 1995).

infrastructure of this beloved home includes the levels of living organisms (bacteria, fungi, even viruses), the world of chemistry (natural and human-made molecules), and the world of physics (atoms, waves, photons, quarks, etc.). The details of a beloved earth offer an awesome intricacy and complexity, as well as a frail and beautiful set of networks, all of which we are called to love. And the ecological beloved community needs enough lovers of this earth who make it their beloved in order to save it.[82]

A Final Word about Lost Causes

Josiah Royce believed that lost causes bring out the best in us. Such causes are not hopeless, but they do seem lost because of their scope or magnitude. Royce believed that, rather than giving up on lost causes, one should be loyal to them since they inspire the highest moral commitment. Considering environmental justice and restoration as a lost (yet not hopeless) cause has the power to spark our moral imaginations. The scope of the cause is so vast that no individual can grasp all of its complexity, and the cause will be achieved over several lifetimes and across all disciplines of human labor. Dedicating ourselves to the cause of the environment does speak to our highest moral commitments and our grandest dreams of human and nonhuman well-being. As an ecological Beloved Community committed to this cause, we remember a world that has slipped away and we hope for a better world in the future. And perhaps we find some motivation for our dedication in the experience of natural beauty.

To better consider natural beauty in the development of a theological aesthetics of nature, and thus to understand natural beauty

---

82. Frank M. Oppenheim, correspondence with the author, 11/13/2012.

more deeply as a source of religious insight, I turn in the next chapter to the work of Andy Goldsworthy. His art, using found objects in nature, has the power to help us see the beauty that surrounds us and, more importantly, how we are connected to that beauty. This is the contribution of the artist.

3

———

Nature Revealed

Religious Insight in the Art of Andy Goldsworthy

The camera pans slowly along a babbling brook, enticing the film's viewers with the gentle sounds of water traveling over river stones. The scene is picturesque and calm. The banks of the brook are lush, shady. Stones covered with moss line pathways for the water as it meanders to its next turn. The camera comes slowly upon a small waterfall, with no more than a two-foot drop into a pool below that eventually rejoins the stream. As it pauses on that waterfall, there is suddenly a faint tint of red to be seen as the water makes its descent. That hint of red grows stronger, more vibrant, until the water looks as if it has turned to blood, as if it has come to life. The shock of color comes as a surprise. As the red water joins the stream below, the pigment reveals complex currents underneath the surface of the water and eventually dissipates.

So opens a scene in the documentary on Andy Goldsworthy's work, "Rivers and Tides."[1] The artist narrates the scene between long stretches of a wordless soundscape. Using few words, Goldsworthy describes how the red in that place is not obvious; this is a place he had worked many times before without noticing the red. The color comes from hard-to-distinguish iron deposits among the other rocks that he grinds for hours into powder. He was surprised to find the pigment, "something so dramatic, so intense, so hidden underneath the skin of the earth," and he is able to surprise the viewer with a sudden infusion of brilliant red in the water.

While he insists that there is a world beyond the limitation of words, and that his art can say much more than words, Goldsworthy attempts to describe what is revealed as the red pigment hits the water. He observes that we tend to think of stone as stable and solid, but in actuality it is fluid. The stone is alive and has a life cycle of solidification and erosion. There is energy within it, though it seems inert; there is life, however slowly that life process moves. His simple act of tossing a ball of red pigment into the water challenges all we thought about rock as lifeless and stable. In countless such examples with stone, wood, ice, even wool, his art has the power to show us what has been there all along.

But if that were the only gift of his art to the viewer, Goldsworthy's work could be reduced to a kind of pastoral sentimentalism, as some of his critics suggest. He is engaged in much more than reclaiming found objects in nature and arranging them in his signature creative, attractive ways. "At the heart of what I do," he explains, "are a growing understanding and a sharpening perception of the land."[2] In other words, not only is Goldsworthy helping his audiences to see the beauty that is already contained in the natural world: his "touch" looks into the heart of nature[3] and opens the door for aesthetic, even

1. Thomas Riedelsheimer, "Rivers and Tides: Andy Goldsworthy Working with Time" [videorecording]. Mediopolis Film with Skyline Productions, Ltd., 2004.
2. Andy Goldsworthy, *Andy Goldsworthy: A Collaboration with Nature* (New York: Abrams, 1990), Introduction.

religious insight at the intersection of human aesthetics and natural beauty. This chapter explores that intersection as a source of religious insight.

While he does not make any overtly religious claims about his work (or his own religious sensibilities), Goldsworthy does have a "deep sense of spirituality."[4] In his own words he describes his art as spiritual, but not mystical. "Mon oeuvre est un art spirituel, mais non mystique, qui perpétue la longue tradition d'un art qui fait voir, sentir et comprendre la nature." (*My work is spiritual but not mystical, art that continues the long tradition of making art in order to see, feel and understand nature.*)[5] He does not engage in what religious scholars might call theological reflection. That is a liberty I will take in this chapter. A methodological disclaimer: I am a theologian treading cautiously into the world of art and art history for the purpose of theological reflection. This chapter is a conversation between the works themselves and beauty as a theological category. I am entering into his discipline to the extent possible because I believe that his art, as an exemplary representation of the larger land art movement, has the power to reveal natural beauty to us in a way that is vital to Christian ecological theology today. Perhaps in this way we can grow in an understanding that redemption in an ecological age must include the human and the natural world, both of which need salvation, and that they are one and the same according to the artist.[6] Perhaps, through the lens of the artist, we can put some words to what Josiah Royce himself longed to say of nature, whose beauty is a source of religious insight.

3. Ibid.

4. William Malpas, *The Art of Andy Goldsworthy: Complete Works* (Maidstone: Crescent Moon, 2005), 262.

5. Catherine Grout, "Une esthétique pragmatique," *Art Press* 192 (juin 1994): 35.

6. Goldsworthy has often made statements such as: "Nature goes beyond what is called countryside—everything comes from the earth." *Andy Goldsworthy*, Introduction.

The Landscapes of Andy Goldsworthy

If the babbling brook scene in "Rivers and Tides" is a good introduction to the works of Goldsworthy, there is a different scene that introduces well the personality of the artist. The scene transpires in his kitchen in Fernside, Penpont in Dumfriesshire, a small Scottish village in a rural area. The British ex-pat is sitting at the table, sipping out of a mug, seemingly gazing off into space. The viewer has the impression that he is thinking of his work for the day before heading outdoors. Meanwhile, his wife, ceramics professor Judith Gregson, is busily multi-tasking, making breakfast and dealing with four energetic children. The noise and the daily demands of children and running a household do not seem to register with Goldsworthy, an introvert already absorbed in his art. At one point in the scene his wife asks him what he's going to do for the day, to which he mockingly replies, as if to a classroom of students or to a reporter, "I work intuitively."[7]

Goldsworthy was not a great student growing up, and he was not admitted to his first choice of art schools. He ended up at Preston Polytechnic in Lancaster, an art college that embraced the *avant garde* of modern art. He was known to skip classes, except for lectures in art history. He often traded class time for being outside and working on the beach. He realized that he needed to document what he was doing for his professors, since his creations would wash away with the tides or succumb to the weather. Thus began his practice of recording his works through photography, a step that would eventually lead to his becoming popular through the sale of books of photographs.

While in art school Goldsworthy was influenced by the pioneers of land art, especially Richard Long, who lectured at Preston. "Land art"

---

7. "Rivers and Tides." Biographical information is from Malpas, *The Art of Andy Goldsworthy*, 27–28.

as a genre has been described and contested in various ways since its inception in the 1960s. Its founders, who include Robert Smithson, Nancy Holt, Richard Long, and Michael Heizer, wanted to free landscape from painting and schmaltzy sentimentalism. Instead of creating decorative placebos for urban angst, land artists sought to aggravate that angst by displaying what had become of the natural world in an industrialized and consumerist age.[8]

Land art as a genre includes forms such as landscape art, earth art, earthworks, nature art, ecological art, installations, gardening, garden architecture, even flower arranging.[9] Some critics suggest that its roots lie in twentieth-century contemporary art, beginning with such works as Duchamp's "ready mades," or *objets trouvés* of surrealism in modern art, as in the works of Andy Warhol. Dismissive critics question whether land art even counts as art rather than craft, a lower category of creativity.

Land art cannot be understood properly as an isolated movement to liberate art from galleries. In *Gender and Aesthetics*, Carolyn Korsmeyer argues that land art is one of several related movements, including feminist art, that emerged simultaneously and synergistically in the 1960s and 1970s. She quotes Peggy Phelan: ". . . feminist art was itself framed by simultaneously occurring art movements and by the discourses that surrounded it. Pop and Conceptual art, Minimalism, Happenings, body art, Land art, photography, experimental film and public art were all vying for attention when feminist art began to be recognized . . . a recognition that was rooted in political awakening."[10] And these movements have much more in common than simply challenging the status quo of the

8. Simon Schama, "The Stone Gardener: A Land Artist Comes to Lower Manhattan," *The New Yorker* 79, no. 27 (September 22, 2003): 126–32, at 128.
9. Malpas, *The Art of Andy Goldsworthy*, 21.
10. Peggy Phelan, "Survey" in Reckitt, *Art and Feminism*, 19, cited in Carolyn Korsmeyer, *Gender and Aesthetics: An Introduction* (New York: Routledge, 2004), 114.

"established art world"—a term I am using to include a hierarchy of art schools, galleries, museums, the market for fine arts, and so on.

Fundamentally, these movements share a critique of Kant's disinterested observer and the Enlightenment idea of the universality of aesthetic values. Adding a feminist critique, Korsmeyer suggests that these movements rebel against what in eighteenth-century France came to be known as *l'homme de goût*, or man of taste and refinement. This man of taste theoretically could appreciate art with developed sensitivities (interestingly, feminine in nature) and refined aesthetic discernment. Such discernment carried implicit presumptions about race, class, and gender. And this arbiter of good taste was implicitly male, thus more capable of reason and of demanding subjects like aesthetics. Looking back now, we can see that this man of taste, like Kant's observer, was never universal nor without gender and location and status.[11]

Korsmeyer insists, and rightly so, that Enlightenment developments in aesthetics are still in use today in the art world, including the contentious idea that aesthetic value is universal, as well as independent of and sometimes outweighing moral assessment. Yet the proponents of these movements from the 1960s and 1970s insist that this is not the case; these movements in particular (though their creators would probably argue the same of art in general) are never amoral. For example, the fact that someone like Goldsworthy does not offer an explicit environmental ethics does not mean that the viewer cannot experience at least a tacit ethics with implications for a morally demanding relationship rather than a dualistic relationship between humanity and nature.

Further, Korsmeyer argues, the impulse to isolate aesthetic qualities from their social location blunts the very power of art.[12]

11. *Gender and Aesthetics*, 46–47.
12. Ibid., 57.

Goldsworthy's work, like that of many of the artists in these movements, has not been curated in the finest museums of modern art or the most prestigious galleries, so the "power" of his art cannot come from prestige granted by the establishment. At the same time his selling of many "coffee table books" reveals this very tension about the judgment of aesthetic value. Does his popularity reveal a kind of power in his art, or does it signal a more pedestrian appeal? The critics are divided.

In "The Art World Divided" below I will discuss the criticisms of land art, and of Goldsworthy's work specifically. What will be clear in that discussion is that there is great division about the quality, value, and meaning of land art. As the critics argue, an interesting question is emerging about land art and related movements. Namely, as artists like Goldsworthy remain in tension with the establishment and create works largely across art disciplines, new discourses emerge. And as they do, critics and art historians are asking the question whether, in the long run, a movement like land art will become its own respected discipline. Sympathetic art historian Manon Regimbald says yes, land art is indeed offering *"la formation de l'épistémè contemporaine."*[13]

Form and Process

Goldsworthy is known around the world for two types of works: ephemeral creations that are transient in nature and both indoor and outdoor permanent installations. He works with stone, wood, ice, sticks, leaves, and anything he can find to create truly fascinating patterns of color and image, from vivid color spectra to black holes or voids nestled in a tree trunk. He creates stone cones, cairns, stone walls and cracking walls of mud, and even restores medieval

13. Manon Regimbald, *D'entre les arts, l'in situ*, Mosaic 31, no. 4 (December 1998), 119.

sheepfolds, as in Cumbria. He restores houses in rural France that once hid those seeking safe harbor during times of war. He uses materials he can find and is considered a low-impact environmental artist. Unlike some more purist land artists, however, he uses technology when needed to cut stone, for example, and also collaborates with professional wallers and other contractors to build permanent installations.

Perhaps the best introduction to the form and process of Goldsworthy's works is the language of the artist himself:

> Movement, change, light, growth and decay are the lifeblood of nature, and the energies that I try to tap through my work. I need the shock of touch, the resistance of place, materials, and weather, the earth as my source. I want to get under the surface. When I work with a leaf, rock, stick, it is not just that material in itself, it is an opening into the process of life within and around it. When I leave it, these processes continue.[14]

Goldsworthy claims that when his work is most successful his "touch" looks into the heart of nature and natural processes, but that on most days he does not even come close. Process and decay or transience are implicit both in nature and in his creations.[15] He does not seek to create against natural processes but within them—which, of course, makes curators like those at the Getty Research Institute very nervous when he creates a circular indoor installation with clay slabs that continue to crack unpredictably long after he leaves. This seems to both amuse and intrigue the artist.[16]

Though Goldsworthy uses repeating forms (e.g. ball, spiral, patch, line, arch, spire, snake, circle),[17] his genius and originality lie in

---

14. Goldsworthy, *Andy Goldsworthy,* Introduction.
15. While transience is a theme he embraces in his art, it is not his stance or attitude toward art in general. See ibid.
16. Thomas Reese, "Andy Goldsworthy's New Ruins," 25–34 in *Mortality Immortality? The Legacy of 20th Century Art* (Los Angeles: Getty Conservation Institute, 1998), 27.
17. *Andy Goldsworthy*, ibid.

creatively fresh interpretations of those forms in unique settings. He will often visit a site over and over again, deciding what to make there, be it in the North Pole or some other international site or in the open land around his village. "The best of my work," he says, "sometimes the result of much struggle when made, appears so obvious that it is incredible I didn't see it before. It was there all the time."[18] He seems to take particular delight in his urban installations, which often go unrecognized, as if they are part of the urban fabric that people may have passed many times before noticing it. His intention with walls, arches, and cones in such installations is to remind the viewer (with subtlety perhaps) that even the city comes from the earth, and though it may seem inert, it too has a life process like that of the stones he has shaped there. When he is not being subtle he will place giant snowballs on city streets and watch commuters pass them with curious expressions, forming a living river of people passing by something transient amidst the buildings they incorrectly perceive to be permanent. Even stones and cities, according to the artist, have a slow-motion ephemerality, in some way contrasted and revealed by the high-speed melting of a snowball on concrete and asphalt.[19] Oliver Lowenstein suggests that with such works Goldsworthy wrestles with the question of a city's ecological equilibrium, a question that is alien to current mainstream British artists.

There is certainly an element of performance art in Goldsworthy's process. At times that has been explicit. He once collaborated with a choreographer, offering a simultaneous dance on stage, a film that featured him making a clay wall playing on a screen behind the dancers, and an actual clay wall audibly cracking behind the

18. Ibid.
19. Oliver Lowenstein, "Natural Time and Human Experience: Andy Goldsworthy's Dialogue with Modernity," *Sculpture* 22, no. 5 (June 2003): 34–39, at 37–38.

audience.[20] This is clearly an artist who does not want to be boxed into a category. If he is doing an installation indoors at a museum he will invite employees to participate (though they often decline for liability's sake), and he will be "on view" for an audience during the creation of the work. This performance art aspect supports Regimbald's assertion that land artists offer a truly new interdisciplinarity and are not so easily defined as perhaps they were when the movement began.

What completes the artist's process, finally, is the interaction with people. Land art draws people out into landscapes they might not otherwise see. It thus provides a mediated experience of place that may foster appreciation and even preservation.[21] This interaction is one that Goldsworthy particularly welcomes because of his fascination with the historical interplay of nature, humans, and animals in a given place, such as the sheepfolds of Cumbria. Shepherds once had access to common land, but that land was partitioned as part of a long history of privatization. Britain has a particular history of conflicts over public rights to land, enclosures, and trespassing (which is one reason why Goldsworthy moved to Scotland, where he could have more access to open land). The interplay of natural and social histories in landscape will be discussed in "Rethinking Landscape" below. Given this lineage, he embraces the idea that an outdoor work is not finished until a path is made to, through, or around it so that people can interact and connect with the work. Fortunately, with his growing fame Goldsworthy has been allowed increasingly to create work on private land with some public access.

20. Ibid., 38–39.
21. John Beardsley, "Foreword," in Molly Donovan, Tina Fiske, and Andy Goldsworthy, *The Andy Goldsworthy Project* (New York: Thames & Hudson, 2012), at xii–xv.

The Art World Divided

The spectrum of critique of Goldsworthy's work is almost as breathtaking as the works themselves. The first challenge for reviewers is how to classify his work. Is he a sculptor, an environmental sculptor, a photographer . . . ? One demeaning review claimed that his work belongs to the craft of those who transform nature into humanized nature, as do cooks, gardeners, architects, and flower arrangers. The underlying criticism in comments like this is that Goldsworthy is more of a craftsman than an artist. He argues that he is both, which I think is a valid response.[22] Having worked on a farm in his youth, he respects craftspeople for their skill and welcomes collaborations.

The list of such reviews is quite long. He has been called a glamorist of nature, an ornamentalist, and a hunter of beauty (a particular insult in contemporary art), and it has been said that he "fiddles around with nature."[23] He has been accused of all of the following:

- Avoidance of political issues
- Romanticizing the natural world
- Conservatism
- Nostalgia
- Escapism
- Self-indulgence
- Elitism
- Repetition and lack of imagination

22. Stefan Beyst, "Andy Goldsworthy: The Beauty of Creation," at en.wikipedia.org/wiki/Andy_Goldsworthy. Accessed 24 June 2007.
23. Schama, "The Stone Gardener," 130.

- Lack of formal experimentation

- Oversimplification of subjects

- Not wrestling with the sublime (just twigs and rocks)[24]

That is a formidable list of faults, some of which seem founded while others appear unnecessarily hostile. Goldsworthy appears to be a popular target, perhaps due to his popularity and success. In a curious chapter about spirituality and sculpture, William Malpas makes some wild assumptions about Goldsworthy's work. He names Goldsworthy's aesthetics as neo-pagan, shamanic, American Indian, Maori, pantheistic, nature worshiping, New Age, and primally animistic because he once heard the artist lecture on energy in his work. Because Goldsworthy uses spirals, he is apparently connected to ancient goddess cults. Moreover, Malpas claims, he eroticizes his touch with stone and is one of the most "feminine" of land artists, who conceal the violence of their gestures.[25] In my research on Goldsworthy's lectures, articles, and artist notebooks I have not encountered these terms or conclusions in the words of the artist himself. Such reviews raise an interesting question about the intention or vision of the artist in tension with layers of interpretation placed on the art (and artist) once the art is no longer in the hands of the artist.

But the fact that Goldsworthy has not been shown in the Tate Collection, the pantheon of British modernism, raises a more serious question. Simon Schama offers possible reasons: Goldsworthy's work is morally intense; he has a devotion to both work and craft; he follows his scientific curiosity as a guiding principle; he engages intelligently the long history of land use; and finally, he has a keen instinct for the baroque hyperbole of the natural world. These

24. Malpas, *The Art of Andy Goldsworthy*, 38.
25. Ibid., 261–262.

qualities are not those the Tate would judge as inherent in fine modern art. Schama explains that, fundamentally, Goldsworthy values clarity over irony and northern plainness over metropolitan chic.[26] It seems that this tension between the judges of modern art and his own work began as early as his difficulty in art college and continues to this day.

So what of the positive reviews? Goldsworthy is hailed by some for many of the very things for which he is dismissed by others. His work is located in the popular vernacular, not postmodern jargon, which, to his own pleasure, brings a wider audience to his art. According to Lenore Metrick, Goldsworthy's art cannot be reduced to nostalgia. It comprehends and even exploits the human propensity to idealize nature. And while his work can seem to dehistoricize the past (as seen in his preference for rural sites), he creates something of a "mythic present" that is profound and that includes the long history of a given place, longer than what we normally conceptualize. Part of why he is so popular is that his work tends to be seen as a visionary transmission directly from nature itself, but that is the result of the skill with which Goldsworthy makes artifice appear naturalized. Above all, Metrick asserts that his works remind us that we create culture from constant negotiations with the still-present past in a particular place and through mediation with fragments of nature.[27] This is why the idea of landscape must be renegotiated, and Goldsworthy offers us the gift of that very question.

It is clear that the art world is divided about whether Goldsworthy is a genius or someone who makes money from selling pictures of rocks he has rearranged. So he is not a perfect candidate to represent singularly the land art movement for the sake of a work of theology.

---

26. Schama, "The Stone Gardener," 131.
27. Lenore Metrick, "Disjunctions in Nature and Culture: Andy Goldsworthy," *Sculpture* 22, no. 5 (June 2003): 29–33.

Perhaps, therefore, I need to justify my selection. I first came across his work in a class on theological aesthetics. The professor flashed a slide on the wall: a picture of stones that had been cut and shaped into the image of a nautilus, with a crack running through in a spiral. It was beautiful, and I was stunned. I have had that same reaction over and over again to Goldsworthy's works. When I see the images of wood, stone, ice, even wool, I am moved, and that moment of being so moved is the subject of this book in general. What is going on theologically in that moment? It is clearly something more than pretty stones in a pattern or sunlight shining through an arch made of ice. It has to do with the connection between the beauty already given and the beauty created in collaboration with human hands. It is not simply that Goldsworthy reveals to his audience what is already there in nature. What is revealed is a profound connection between that beauty and a full range of human creativity and emotions, from longing and melancholy to joy. That moment is a moment of religious insight.

Rethinking Landscape

In a course on ecological theology I once asked the students to play a word association game and offer anything that came to mind in relation to the term "landscape." The responses included the following: pastures, a beach and ocean scene, wilderness, non-urban, the Hudson River School painters, bucolic, gardens, and the kind of art you find in hotel rooms. It was a fairly bland list, but the theme running through the answers was fairly clear. We presume that landscape means more or less anculture-free or at least culture-minimal space.

Some of Goldsworthy's detractors assume that when he goes out onto a deserted beach and makes a cone of slate, or if he travels to the North Pole to make arches out of ice, he is falling into some kind of naïve sentimentalism about landscape that is virtually absent of human culture. This is where the charge of elitism enters: his works are nothing more than those of an artist with nothing but spare time and financial freedom to go to expensive wild places and make pretty things. Alternatively, the critical argument goes something like this: he is attempting to assuage middle-class guilt about destruction of the environment by creating and photographing amelioristic images of nature that is still intact.[28]

But Goldsworthy insists that the social and the natural are not mutually exclusive. In Britain, where he was formed as an artist, there is no untouched landscape; land art has always dealt there with social history as well as natural space. In fact, Goldsworthy is particularly interested in those intersections. He welcomes collaborations with wallers and shepherds, for example, and considers memories of human and animal occupation when he works in a space.[29]

So what if we consider the idea of landscape without a nature/culture dualism? This is the direction in which Goldsworthy points us, and it is a critical concept to consider in ecological theology generally and for a theological aesthetics of nature specifically.

In *Landscape and Memory*, historian Simon Schama offers a brilliant consideration of the human/landscape relationship. He suggests that every landscape—forest, river, mountain, city—is a work of the mind and a repository of the memories and obsessions of the people who gaze upon it. We look at nature and see history and myth. Landscape, in fact, is a work of the mind. Its scenery is built up as much from layers of memory as from layers of rock. All ecosystems, not merely industrialized areas, have been modified by human culture.[30]

28. Malpas, *The Art of Andy Goldsworthy*, 38.
29. Schama, "The Stone Gardener," 131.
30. Simon Schama, *Landscape and Memory* (New York: Knopf, 1995), 5–6.

Take, for example, certain fathers of modern environmentalism, Henry David Thoreau and John Muir. Both saw the potential of wilderness and promised that "in the wilderness would be the preservation of the world."[31] The operating presumption in that assertion is that the wilderness out there awaiting discovery would be the antidote to the poisons of city life. This was the promise of Walden Pond. Think, too, of Yosemite as the holy park of the West, a place of rebirth for one's soul. But the healing wilderness, Schama suggests, was as much a product of culture's craving and framing as any other imagined garden. Think of Ansel Adams's photographs on many city-dwellers' walls. His works suggest an absence of human presence, but of course the very act of identifying and photographing the place presupposes our presence and "the heavy cultural backpacks we lug on the trail."[32]

Schama's argument is that wildernesses do not identify themselves. Even the landscapes we suppose to be the most free of culture turn out, on closer inspection, to be its product. This should not be a cause for guilt and sorrow, Schama concludes. Even while we acknowledge the human impact on ecology, this is a cause for celebration and inspiration, and ultimately for responsibility. The word "landscape" shares roots with the German *Landschaft*, which signifies a unit of human occupation or jurisdiction, not just a pleasing site to enjoy.[33]

In 1938, René Magritte gave a lecture on a painting he called "La condition humaine." The image is of a painting that has been superimposed over the view it depicts through a window, so that the painting and the view are continuous and indistinguishable. "We see it [the landscape] as being outside ourselves even though it is only a mental representation of what we experience on the inside."[34] In

31. Ibid., 7.
32. Ibid.
33. Ibid., 10.
34. Ibid., 12.

other words, we experience beauty only when we see it in our minds first. Land artists have found this idea offensive and have tried to dissolve the ego within the natural process. They aim for a minimally mediated experience. Landscape for land artists has become anti-landscape, or at least anti-museum. But their work, according to Schama, rarely escapes the condition they criticize. A camera (used by Goldsworthy and others) is not different from a paintbrush because neither offers a possibility of separating the ego from the landscape.

The hope, according to Schama, and I think implicitly according to Goldsworthy, is that the history of landscape in the West is not just a "mindless race toward a machine-driven universe." This is not the whole story, and we are not trapped by the engine of our self-destruction. To grasp this we must reject nature/culture dualism and see the strength in the connection between them. It is not the case that we need new creation myths to repair the environment, as some suggest; rather, we need to rediscover the ways we already have of viewing landscape as full of life, myth, and culture.

The intersection of human creativity and natural beauty in Goldsworthy's work is a glimpse of this potential rejection of nature/culture dualism. It is in keeping with Aldo Leopold's ethic in *A Sand County Almanac*, which names a thing as right when "it tends to preserve the integrity, stability, and beauty of the biotic community."[35] This community must include the human and natural world, which can be seen as a unity if landscape is properly redefined.

Aesthetics, Natural Beauty, and Religious Insight

Chapter two explored natural beauty as a source of religious insight, attempting to develop Josiah Royce's claim that natural beauty should

---

35. Beardsley, "Foreword," *The Andy Goldsworthy Project,* xii.

be included among those sources, though he himself did not put many words to nature-beauty or art. Recall the thunderstorm as an experience of the sublime, a power beyond us that helps us to understand our need for salvation. This is unlike a private, mystical experience; Royce's philosophy suggests that, along with other sources of religious insight, such an experience of natural beauty can draw us into a community of others dedicated to loyalty, a community devoted to ecological restoration and the well-being of the beloved community. In that process of illumination we glimpse our own need for salvation, with a broadened understanding of sin that includes ecological destruction, and learn to live our lives for higher aims and thus find their ultimate meaning. The final fulfillment of this process for Royce was the Beloved Community, now an ecological beloved community as a community of memory and hope, ever interpreting meaning into the future. Chapter two concluded with the question of how better to understand natural beauty now that a process of philosophical interpretation is in place.

How to put words to the experience of natural beauty is a theological question. The experience somehow has to do with ultimate meaning and with human nature and culture. It has to do with experiencing creation in relation to a God who created this world with natural beauty, and not a different world devoid of such beauty. It presents the troubling question: why do we simultaneously crave experiences of natural beauty and destroy that possibility? In reverse, what is the connection between ecological salvation (saving beauty) and human redemption (beauty saving)? This is precisely where the land artist comes in.

First, in recalling the history of theological reflection on natural beauty, we see that the beauty of creation has played many roles:

- reorienting and consoling pilgrims on their earthly journey (ancient)

- serving as a bridge to divine beauty, or at least a starting point on the mystical ascent (medieval)

- serving as an agent of conversion and a reflection of God's glory (modern)

- reemerging as a needed subject in theological discourse (postmodern)

Through all of these roles, while weathering dramatic shifts in religious and philosophical thought, beauty has maintained a place within soteriology. Even with all the historical shifts in conceptualization, the central idea that the experience of natural beauty is in some way redemptive has prevailed.

From Royce we understand that such an experience draws us redemptively into community, into a Beloved Community reimagined in light of ecological concerns. The artist in this case study, Andy Goldsworthy, adds another dimension to what this book tries to articulate about the experience of natural beauty. Goldsworthy helps us to see a connection between nature and culture rather than a dualism, to see the link between natural beauty (divine creativity) and human creativity. The two work as one. The beauty of the one is related to the beauty of the other. The diminishment of one is related to the diminishment of the other. This is the connection between ecological and human redemption. Goldsworthy helps us to see the beauty that is already before us and that we crave. In adding human aesthetics we are able to see how natural beauty helps us to thrive, even draws us into a community of environmental ethics. And this connection, once revealed, helps us to see its negation as well. The destruction of natural beauty diminishes us and what we can co-create. In an ecological age this is a much-needed addition to the articulation of human sin. We are destroying something we need.

If Royce was right that religious insight, including beauty as a source, is insight into the need and way of salvation, and if Alejandro García-Rivera was right that theological aesthetics recognizes in the experience of the beautiful a religious dimension, then we must have a theological aesthetics of nature for ecological theology. That is the subject of the next chapter.

A Theological Aesthetics of Nature

Camp Mitchell, the retreat center on top of Petit Jean Mountain in Arkansas, and the place with the open-air chapel featuring a cross that appears suspended against the landscape below, was the site of a recent parish retreat for my congregation. Such a lovely setting away from the city seemed like the perfect location for a consideration of the good life, the theme of the retreat. We discussed cultural messages we receive about what will make us happy, such as worldly success and material wealth and acquisition. In contrast, we discussed the ancient Greek idea of *eudaimonia* (εὐδαιμονία), often translated as "happiness," a definition that does not quite capture its depth. We drew on this idea as expressed by Aristotle in *The Nicomachean Ethics*,[1] in which he discusses this happiness not as ease of life or having wealth, but rather as human flourishing at its deepest level. We considered a lengthy list of virtues and the ideal of living a balanced life according to the mean between extremes of such virtues,

---

1. Aristotle, *The Nicomachean Ethics*, trans. Christopher Rowe (Oxford: Oxford University Press, 2002).

including such things as assertiveness, compassion, and discipline. Taking the idea of *eudaimonia*, contrasted to what American culture might say about happiness, I asked the group to create a definition of a Christian good life.

Participants came up with several components of the Christian good life. The list included regular disciplines such as regular attendance at worship, leisure time with family and friends and the church community, meaningful work, time for study, charitable giving and volunteering in the community, and health of body and spirit. Finally, perhaps inspired by the setting, the group added time in nature. People described daily routines of walking on the Arkansas River Trail, gardening, birdwatching, or returning to a beautiful spot with some regularity. Some, especially those who do not have a regular practice of being outdoors and who find it difficult to make the time for it, expressed a longing for these kinds of experiences.

Everyone agreed that experiencing natural beauty is an important dimension of our makeshift definition of the Christian good life, and so we tried to put language to why that is the case. One woman said that our souls need it. Another offered that he experiences God in nature. Everyone was able to recall a time outdoors that was somehow spiritually significant. People described such experiences as restorative, peaceful, necessary, relaxing, and healing. There was certainly an echo of the Transcendentalist idea that nature is somehow an antidote to the poisons of modern urban life.

This book is an exploration of such moments, when the aesthetic and the religious meet in the experience of natural beauty. But, as Alejandro García-Rivera insisted repeatedly in class lectures on theological aesthetics, this is more than a question of spirituality.[2] We are searching for a theological understanding of the relationship

Relationship / World Created with Natural Beauty ← human creatures made to experience the Beauty

2. Lectures, Alejandro García-Rivera, GTU, fall and spring, 2002–2003.

between a world created with natural beauty and human creatures created to experience such beauty. Conversely, why it is that such creatures destroy the very thing they crave? A theological aesthetics of nature addresses this question, naming beauty as a source of religious insight, and it offers, even requires, an integral view of redemption for an ecological age, redemption that includes both the human and the natural world.

A Theological Aesthetics of Nature—Locating the Work

We recall Plato's dictum, χαλεπὰ τὰ καλά, "beautiful things are difficult."[3] Josiah Royce wrote, "As to nature-beauty, I am, and must remain, naïve, ignorant,—at best childlike."[4] Centuries apart, two great minds had difficulty putting language to the experience of beauty. Add to this innate challenge the overarching narrative of beauty offered by Wladyslaw Tatarkiewicz, in which the Great Theory of Beauty changes across the centuries and finally experiences a severe decline in the modern period as beauty is relegated to the subjective realm and to matters of taste.[5] Speaking of the beautiful is more difficult now than ever before, yet beauty is experiencing a resurgence across disciplines and in Christian theology in particular. This project emerges out of the growing field of theological aesthetics.

This book is also rooted in ecological theology. Beginning in the 1970s, the field of ecological theology emerged as theologians undertook the task of reconceiving every area of Christian theology in light of environmental concerns. Today ecological theology is

---

3. Plato, *Greater Hippias*, 304.
4. John Clendenning, ed., *The Letters of Josiah Royce* (Chicago: University of Chicago Press, 1970), 577–78.
5. Wladyslaw Tartarkiewicz, *A History of Ideas: An Essay in Aesthetics* (Warsaw: Polish Scientific Publishers, 1980), chap. 4.

a global movement that represents a vast body of interdisciplinary literature touching every area of systematic theology. The methods and contexts are varied and the sources far-reaching. In an introductory course on "Greening North American Christianity" at the Church Divinity School of the Pacific in Berkeley in the spring of 2005, I had the opportunity to explore this rich, varied terrain within the North American context with my students. We began with a few "classics" of ecology, such as Rachel Carson's wake-up call about the use of DDT in *Silent Spring* (1962), Aldo Leopold's land ethic in *A Sand County Almanac* (1949), and Lyn White's scathing view of Christianity as the world's most anthropocentric religion and the cause of environmental harm.[6] From there we moved through surveys of the historical roots of U.S. environmentalism and attitudes toward nature, the work of avowed ecological theologians, environmental ethics, ecofeminism, "green" biblical exegesis, official church statements and publications on the environment, and poetry and theology ranging from Augustine's *City of God* to Annie Dillard's *Holy the Firm* as the works of "green visionaries." Bringing their own insights to the material, students critically examined a range of topics that included Christian ethical responses to the biodiversity crisis, the creation of an adult formation program on ecological theology for use in local Catholic parishes, and a study of the possibility of greening North American theological education. In short, the topics explored in this introductory course offered a snapshot of a theological movement that seeks to address, as one voice among many, perhaps the most complex, profound theoretical and practical questions humanity has ever faced. The central theological *loci* of God, creation, humanity, and soteriology must be reexamined in light of environmental destruction.

6. Lyn White, "The Historical Roots of Our Ecologic Crisis," *Science*, n.s.155, no. 3767 (1967): 1203–07.

There is, of course, no single definition of what makes theology "ecological." Ethicist Dieter Hessel offers a helpful schema of seven areas that are common within Christian ecological theologies:

- The reexamination of scripture and tradition and refocusing affirmations and ethics in ecologically sound terms

- The exploration of the relationship between cosmology, spirituality, and morality

- Critique and response to disastrous assumptions underlying modern philosophy, religion, technology, and politics

- The requirement of theology and praxis, sacramental and covenantal commitment for a sustainable community

- Reconstruction of affirmations about the categories of systematic theology: God, Christ, sin, redemption, the world, eschatology, etc.

- The emergence and transformation of Christian ecological virtue ethics that lead to praxis and justice for all

- An emphasis on human obligations that express respect and care for the earth as God's creation, while seeking justice for biodiversity and humankind.[7]

Hessel's list demonstrates how classical theological questions are being asked anew in light of environmental concerns. Given the complexity of such issues, is there a place for beauty in the conversation? There have been glimpses of beauty in the work of various ecological theologians, from Thomas Berry to Sallie McFague. Yet there have been few sustained examinations of beauty as a singular focus.

7. Dieter Hessel, "Christianity and Ecology: Wholeness, Respect, Justice, Sustainability," *Earth Ethics* 10, no. 1 (Fall 1998), 8–10.

[Handwritten annotation: Justice = creating "Right Relationships" Beauty = incarnation + measure of relational integrity.]

One such emergent voice is that of Brazilian ecofeminist theologian Ivone Gebara, who asks, in "Yearning for Beauty," what beauty and justice have to do with our salvation. She answers: everything. "If justice is fundamentally about creating right relationships, beauty is in many ways the incarnation and measure of the integrity of those relationships. It is a kind of aesthetic love, an invitation to nurture the creativity and integrity of every created thing. It is an invitation to salvation."[8] These words suggest that the experience of the beautiful in creation has something to say to our souls, and the message is of great importance not only for our knowledge of God but also for how we ought to live. I believe she is articulating something similar to Josiah Royce's understanding of religious insight, as that which helps us to understand the highest aims of human life and draws us redemptively into a community dedicated to higher causes. Today one of the highest aims is to work for ecological redemption, a category that contains the social as well as the natural world. And theologically speaking, our own redemption is connected to the ecological, as the experience of natural beauty teaches.

A Theological Aesthetics of Nature Thus Far

The central premise of a theological aesthetics of nature is that the experience of natural beauty is a source of religious insight into the need and way of human salvation, offering an integral view of redemption that includes both the human and the natural world.

The experience of natural beauty has to do with ultimate meaning and the highest aims of human life. A theological aesthetics seeks to understand experiencing creation in relation to a God who created

8. Ivone Gebara, "Yearning for Beauty," *The Other Side* (July/August 2003), 24–25.

this world with natural beauty, and not a different world devoid of such beauty. It demands that we ask how we ought to live in more sustainable ways. It presents the troubling question: why do we simultaneously crave experiences of natural beauty and destroy that possibility? A theological aesthetics explores the connection between ecological salvation (saving beauty) and human redemption (beauty saving). In conjunction with the saving work of Christ, a theological aesthetics seeks to understand beauty and its diminishment as a window into our need for salvation in the first place. It offers a sense of sin in connection to the beauty we crave yet destroy. Questions of human sin can no longer be addressed apart from ecological destruction. The experience of natural beauty can both convict us and inspire us to work for natural redemption.

The first step to articulating a theological aesthetics of nature is to recall the history of theological reflection on natural beauty, in which we see that the beauty of creation has played many roles. Despite beauty's post-Enlightenment decline, it still offers a lens for theological reflection. Such a lens is greatly needed in light of the destruction of the beauty of creation.

The second step in the articulation of a theological aesthetics of nature is the development of a theory of interpretation for experiencing beauty. From Royce we learn that such an experience of natural beauty offers us religious insight into the need and way of salvation and draws us redemptively into a reimagined community. The land art of Andy Goldsworthy adds a third dimension, helping us to see a continuity between nature and culture, landscape and art, wilderness and urban life, rather than dualisms. He shows us a connection between natural beauty (divine creativity) and human creativity, the two interrelated and working as one. Here we glimpse the connection between ecological and human redemption. Adding human aesthetics enables us to see how natural beauty helps us to thrive, even draws us into a community of environmental concern. The connection, once revealed, helps us to see its negation as well: how the destruction of natural beauty diminishes us and what we co-create. In our human sinfulness we are destroying something we need, destroying one of our sources of religious insight.

The following themes of the cross in the American wilderness, the community of the beautiful, and the cultivation of a sense of beauty help to develop the three key elements of the argument thus far.

The Cross in the American Wilderness

In chapter one, I traced the history of theological reflection on natural beauty from ancient Greece to the modern period. Yet there is a particular historical moment in American history that is foundational to how we in the North American context understand natural beauty even today and thus deserves its own consideration. The nineteenth century in America witnessed a tremendous shift in attitude toward wilderness. Perhaps it was the discovery of giant sequoias in California, trees that appeared immense and somehow sacred, even Christ-like to those who beheld them.[9] Perhaps it was the Transcendentalist romanticism of places like Walden Pond, a train ride away from demoralizing civilization and a place of rebirth and purity. Perhaps it was the influence of the artists of the Hudson River School such as Thomas Cole and Frederick Church, who played with light and shadows in grand landscapes of danger and redemption, often with a figure of a cross bathed in light yet dwarfed by majestic surroundings.[10]

9. Simon Schama, *Landscape and Memory* (New York: Vintage Books, 1995), 185–186.
10. Elizabeth Kornhauser, "Introduction," *Hudson River School: Masterworks from the Wadsworth Atheneum Museum of Art* (New Haven: Yale University Press, 2003).

Simon Schama traces this history and suggests that the shift in question was a movement from equating the forest with pagan darkness and profanity to discovering "pristine" wilderness as a sanctuary and place of holy asylum. He says of the reconceived forest: "Its foliage trickles with sunlight; its waters run sweet and clear. It is the tabernacle of liberty, ventilated by the breeze of holy freedom and suffused with the golden radiance of providential benediction."[11]

Some of this shift can be attributed to western expansion and the discovery of extraordinarily beautiful places like Yosemite, many of which would become national parks in the nineteenth and twentieth centuries. But this shift did not lend itself wholeheartedly to environmental preservation. In a fascinating study of the legacy of Protestantism in affecting American natural history, Mark Stoll traces how people's religious thinking about nature, and religious thought in general, have affected the natural world. The former, he argues, has an explicit and the latter an implicit effect on nature.[12]

Stoll argues that for Puritan settlers the wilderness and their place within it had many meanings: a refuge, a gathering place for an army of saints, a place of testing, the means of God's providence, a haven for the devil's minions, the site of the new Jerusalem and the new Eden, a place of no history and no authorities to inhibit the creation of a godly nation.[13] Add to this list of meanings the context of the rise of industrial capitalism mixed with Calvinism and we find that the "Puritan road to sanctification was paid for by ecological degradation."[14] On the one hand, wilderness offered cathedrals of beauty that displayed the glory of God and could restore the soul. On the other hand, the Protestant work ethic demanded

---

11. Schama, *Landscape and Memory*, 201.
12. Mark Stoll, *Protestantism, Capitalism, and Nature in America* (Albuquerque: University of New Mexico Press, 1997), x.
13. Ibid., 69.
14. Ibid., 34.

resource exploitation as religious duty. If idleness was sinful and work blessed, the constant use of natural materials for industrialization was required. Simply stated, the roots of environmental destruction as well as environmental preservation in the American context are the same. Calvinism on these shores demanded both. The work ethic, suspicion of Catholic sacramentalism, anti-authoritarianism, and the ideal of limited government all have deep roots in an early culture that saw the wilderness as simultaneously glorious and utilitarian. This deep conflict of interests remains today.

Gender   It should be noted that the historical shift in the nineteenth century is also a gendered history. This period saw the emergence of the "cult of true womanhood," in which the private and public spheres were split and gendered. Work outside the home was masculine and morally suspect. The home was a feminine refuge from the outside and was deemed passive, tender, nurturing, spiritual, and moral. This cultural development was mapped onto nature as well; wilderness was seen as masculine, while nature (parks, gardens, landscapes, etc.) was feminine. Romanticism deemed nature (not too wild) as virgin territory, an escape from a sinful man's world.[15] Traces of this gendered history can be seen today in the environmental movement. The moral urgency of the movement is often framed in terms of temperance and asceticism, (feminine) virtues higher than those of the (masculine) industrial culture.

Understanding natural beauty as a source of religious insight is in many ways a meditation on the popular nineteenth-century image of the cross in the wilderness, and it completes the study in chapter one of the history of theological reflection on natural beauty. It is continuous with the premise that the natural world is somehow restorative and purifying of our moral life. The cross in the landscape is a statement today on human sinfulness, especially as the grandeur

15. Ibid., 45–49.

of nature is compromised through capitalism or domesticated for our use. The cross against the backdrop of beauty stands to convict our appetites and to inspire our highest ideals. Perhaps the more deeply we understand this as both our heritage and a moral imperative for today the more inspired we will be to understand our own redemption as integrated with ecological redemption.

Community of the Beautiful

In chapter two, I explored Josiah Royce's understanding of religious insight and his somewhat hidden aesthetics to develop his sense that nature-beauty could be a source of such insight. I then turned to the community of interpretation, reconceived as the ecological Beloved Community. This community borrows the land ethic from Aldo Leopold and the partnership ethic of Carolyn Merchant to envision a community of interpretation that is not limited to an anthropocentric perspective.

In the nineteenth century Charles Peirce returned to the study of signs, developing a metaphysics that García-Rivera called a "community of the true." Royce, in studying Peirce, advocated a community of the good, a community of interpreters dedicated to loyalty and to higher causes. García-Rivera developed the idea of a community of the beautiful (to which this project is indebted), a community that, in cultivating the spiritual senses, responds to the call of beauty that is revelatory of a source, creator, and bestower of beauty. He describes this interpretive community as follows:

> The Glory of the Lord returns as praise and thanksgiving because the Glory of the Lord is a community that has caught sight of a marvelous vision, a universe of justice emerging from the community's experience of divine Beauty, the "lifting up the lowly." Such a community counts as members the sun and stars, the dead and the living, the angels and

the animals, and, of course, the marvelous yet lowly human creature. Together, in their splendid differences, these individuals give witness of God's power not only to give life but also to ordain it, not only to grant existence but also to order it. As such, these individuals also give witness to the reality of certain relationships, realities held in common, realities that know little of the subject-object split that plagues our understanding today. These realities, whose commonality has its source in God's ordaining power, eschew what has become in our day an iconoclastic view of redemption. Redemption, in light of God's ordaining power, is less a state of mere existence or an invisible inner reality than an ordained existence, a common reality in the midst of marvelous differences, a community where the invisible becomes visible by the power of a bold and daring spiritual imagination which makes manifest communities of Truth, Goodness, and, above all, the Beautiful.[16]

Here García-Rivera eloquently tried to capture the movement of his heart as experienced in the Latin Church of the Americas, communities in which he discovered an embrace of beauty, art, relationship, and justice. Margaret Miles has suggested that the idea of a community of the beautiful has the potential to offer a foundation for constructive theology that is comprehensive enough to incorporate various theologies of liberation. "Founding such theologies on theological aesthetics has the potential to overcome divisions between theory and practice, ideas and liturgies, spirit and matter."[17] García-Rivera attempted to reclaim the term "transcendentals," and especially beauty as a transcendental (and "the beautiful" to denote beauty that is experienced). This is a Roman Catholic *ressourcement* to describe beauty as he did above, namely as the reality held in common and not off limits in a post-Enlightenment world that is suspicious of anything universal. It is an

16. Alejandro García-Rivera, *The Community of the Beautiful* (Collegeville, MN: Liturgical Press, 1999), 195.
17. Margaret Miles, review of García-Rivera, *The Community of the Beautiful, Journal of the American Academy of Religion* 68 (2000): 412–13.

attempt to retrieve beauty from the grip of subjective experience and restore it to its place in theological inquiry.

This idea of the community of the beautiful makes possible a theological aesthetics of nature, which is much more than the sum of individual experiences of pretty places. It is premised on the idea that the experience of natural beauty can be revelatory of a reality held in common, of divine Beauty. This community engages ecological destruction and the disappearance of natural beauty from a liberationist perspective and widens the understanding of sin to include the human capability to destroy beauty. Most importantly, it draws individuals into a community of interpretation dedicated to the cause of ecological redemption as connected to our own. This community remembers the past and interprets together into the future, with hope. There is multifaceted work to be done to achieve this beloved, ecological community, and it has to do with what García-Rivera called cultivating a sense of beauty. The following *Check Images* sections build on the work of chapter three, which explored religious insight in the work of Andy Goldsworthy and the land art movement, inquiring into what the cultivation of a sense of beauty requires.

Cultivating a Sense of Beauty

A theological aesthetics seeks to restore beauty as a locus of theological reflection. García-Rivera argued that through the history of the great theory of beauty we have lost a "sense of beauty" and, as a result, talk of beauty has been rendered increasingly irrelevant and morally impotent in our day. His starting premise is an agreement with Hans Urs von Balthasar, namely, that the only way we have of knowing God is through our senses. García-Rivera's own work sought to reclaim an Augustinian understanding of the cultivation of spiritual senses, noting that the journey or ascent to the divine begins with an experience of the beautiful. He described his project in this succinct statement:

> One of the ways that God is known is Beauty. Beauty is, according to the author of "Divine Names," one of the names of God. As such, whatever participates in Beauty is beautiful and reveals something about God. Beauty, then, not only is divine but its experience, the beautiful, is a way to the divine, a means for the soul to ascend to a blissful union with God . . . . The sense of beauty, then, carries certain theological implications. If Beauty is divine, then the sense of Beauty is key to knowing and loving God, then the sense of Beauty is also the key to the talk of God. In other words, the sense of Beauty is both an aesthetic and a religious experience . . . . The sense of Beauty is, at its heart, the fruit of a spiritual journey and this simple theological observation has been forgotten in our day.[18]

I agree with García-Rivera that we have lost that sense of beauty. The aim of this project is to explore how the experience of natural beauty is redemptive. But, given the decline of beauty, it cannot be a simple trajectory from seeing a pretty place, for example, to a religious insight into the human need for salvation and the connection between human and ecological redemption. I agree that we must once again cultivate a "sense of beauty" to achieve such an insight.

How, then, do we cultivate a sense of beauty? How, in the experience of natural beauty, can we understand theologically the intersection of aesthetic and religious experience without simply collapsing the two into one category? In the case of a theological aesthetics of nature there are several themes to consider that, if taken together, I believe can help us achieve that sense of beauty, or what Thomas Berry called the wonderful sense of the divine through the experience of natural beauty. Building on the study of Andy

18. Alejandro García-Rivera, "The Sense of Beauty and the Talk of God," Graduate Theological Union Distinguished Faculty Lecture, November 13, 2002.

Goldsworthy in chapter three and the contribution of land art, I turn to the questions of a Christian aesthetic, the intersection of aesthetic and religious experience as well as the intersection of the aesthetic and the sacramental, a place for love and passion, and the theme of transience and loss.

From Beauty to the Artist

Wladyslaw Tartarkiewicz has skillfully traced the Great Theory of Beauty and its apparent decline. I have argued that a trajectory of theological reflection on natural beauty survived even through the modern period. And yet, despite that survival, philosophical aesthetics has made it difficult now to speak of beauty as what García-Rivera called a transcendental. Tatarkiewicz suggests that as the modern aesthetics of such key figures as Kant and Hegel have run their course we might be on the verge of another turning point in the great theory of beauty. The modern period brought an end to knowing Kant's sublime, to beauty as a transcendental, and came full stop at the artist. And it brought a kind of hyper-individualism in the world of art. Artists were no longer in relationship to communities, much less religious communities. Abstraction and formalism in art have moved through extremism. Art became entirely self-conscious, as in Marcel Duchamp's ready-mades and the pop images of Andy Warhol.[19]

But perhaps that trajectory has run its course, and a new understanding of art and the artist is emerging. What is refreshing about land art, for example, is an easing of a complete self-consciousness and a return to the value of art in relationship to the viewer. In the consideration, then, of cultivating a sense of beauty,

---

19. It is true, however, as Jane Dillenberger has argued that Warhol had a private, devoutly religious side, as evidenced in his series on the Last Supper. See her *The Religious Art of Andy Warhol* (New York: Continuum, 1998).

there must be a place for the artist. The artist offers a path for aesthetics after the philosophical impasses of the Enlightenment, and that path is the experience of the beautiful that can be shared.

Chapter three explored the work of Andy Goldsworthy as a representative figure of the land art movement. His work helps us to see the connection between natural beauty, or divine creativity, and human creativity. The two operate as one in his work with found objects, revealing through the lens of human aesthetics a beauty that was already there. In experiencing his work we are able to see how the natural beauty we crave helps us to thrive, even drawing us from individual experience of his art into an ecological Beloved Community, and this connection, once revealed, helps us to see its negation also, as Royce insisted we must. The destruction of natural beauty diminishes what we can co-create. We destroy what we need, and we are diminished as we do so. No current understanding of sin is complete without consideration of the loss of natural beauty. This is the insight offered by Goldsworthy, as we see a religious dimension to an aesthetic experience that points us toward the need and the way of salvation.

So if the Great Theory of Beauty ends its story with the decline of beauty as an objective reality, we need the artist to help us regain some of the ancient insights we once gleaned from beauty and to reveal beauty to us in new ways.

A Christian Aesthetic?

Is there anything particularly Christian about experiencing natural beauty? We can answer positively if we consider that experience a locus for theological reflection, particularly as a source of religious insight into soteriological concerns, and also if the experience is rooted in cultivating a sense of beauty as divine, according to a long tradition of theological reflection on natural beauty. But there are two things a possible "Christian aesthetic" is not: it is neither simply a theory of art appreciation nor a matter of taste.

In *Art in Action: Toward a Christian Aesthetic*, Nicholas Wolterstorff attempts to articulate how he as a Christian sees art and the aesthetic dimension of reality. He offers reflections on the arts as someone who stands within the Christian tradition, and he takes what he calls a functional approach to art. "For the aesthetic, as I conceive it, though it does indeed go beyond looks and sounds . . . is nonetheless grounded in looks and sounds."[20] He then offers two pages on beauty before returning to a theory of art appreciation and a canonical presentation of works of art. A theological aesthetics, on the other hand, insists that beauty (whether in the arts or in nature) participates in a divine reality, a reality that is glimpsed as the result of a spiritual journey. Beauty in this world is not self-referential but a sign that participates in the reality to which it points.

important

Another attempt at defining a Christian aesthetic comes from Frank Burch Brown, in his creatively titled *Good Taste, Bad Taste, and Christian Taste*. Brown considers everything from art that makes places sacred to religious kitsch and the issue of quality.[21] The issues around the arts in church is critical for a community of the beautiful, but questions raised about taste, quality, tradition, and innovation are different from the questions of a theological aesthetics, which seeks to understand a religious dimension in the experience of the beautiful.

---

20. Nicholas Wolterstorff, *Art in Action: Toward a Christian Aesthetic* (Grand Rapids: Eerdmans, 1980), 41.
21. Frank Burch Brown, *Good Taste, Bad Taste, and Christian Taste: Aesthetics in Religious Life* (New York: Oxford, 2000).

Aesthetic, Religious, and Sacramental Experience

The cultivation of a sense of beauty is enhanced by a consideration of three different types of experience—aesthetic, religious, and sacramental—all of which overlap in a unique way. These three categories of experience are not interchangeable, yet their intersection is key to understanding a theological aesthetics of nature.

To begin, García-Rivera argued that the perception of beauty must be cultivated; the sense of beauty is not self-evident. It has a revelatory aspect and must be carefully achieved; it is accomplished through a spiritual journey and is intimately related to sanctification.[22] Margaret Miles also speaks of cultivating the ability to see beauty and writes of religion's place between beauty and moral responsibility: "Religion occurs at the intersection of perceived beauty and moral responsibility. Religions seek to describe and actualize, through liturgy, ritual, and devotional practices, a morally demanding vision of beauty. Religions orient and train the eye to recognize what is serious, to see the beauty and integrity of the whole, and to embody particular styles and practices of relationship."[23]

For ecological theology rooted in liturgical traditions, one way of cultivating such moral achievement is through sacramental and liturgical practice. If beauty is a source of religious insight in the Roycean sense, religion and sacramental practice in particular are crucial for the cultivation of the ability to perceive beauty. Such practices train our eyes and moral selves to see the integrity of the whole and to live out that insight in relationship. The sacramental idea that the ordinary, natural creatures of this life, such as bread, wine, water, and oil, can reveal to us the sacred nature of our

22. Garcia-Rivera, "Sense of Beauty."
23. Miles, "Intentions and Effects: Beauty, Pluralism, and Responsibility," *Sewanee Theological Review* 41 (1997): 48–58, at 57.

relationships with one another, with creation, and with the divine, is a profound resource for ecological theology. That the natural world is a vehicle for the holy can assist with the development of a morally demanding vision and understanding of natural beauty, working similarly, in a sense, to Royce's understanding of training in loyalty. I share Sallie McFague's and Rosemary Ruether's conviction that the sacramental tradition has an essential role in healing the ecological crisis.[24] Dorothy McDougall has developed this idea in her work, *The Cosmos as Primary Sacrament*. She argues for an ecological sacramental theology based on the metaphor of the cosmos itself as the primary sacrament. The magnitude of the current ecological crisis demands a fundamental redefinition of what it means to be human, no longer as the apex of creation but rather in the recognition that we exist within an intricate web of cosmic relations.[25] Sacramental practice is a continual reminder of this relational reality.

This idea can also be found in *Super, Natural Christians*, in which Sallie McFague suggests that "Christian practice, loving God and neighbor *as subjects*, as worthy of our love in and for themselves, should be extended to nature . . . we should relate to the entities in nature *in the same basic way* that we are supposed to relate to God and other people—as ends, not means, as subjects valuable in themselves, for themselves."[26] In this book McFague continues her advocacy for a change in attitude or sensibility toward the natural world, this time through the theme of really paying attention to the natural

---

24. Sallie McFague, "An Ecological Christology: Does Christianity Have It?" 29–46 in Dieter Hessel and Rosemary Radford Ruether, eds., *Christianity and Ecology: Seeking the Well-Being of Earth and Humans* (Cambridge, MA: Harvard University Press, 2000); Rosemary Radford Ruether, *Gaia and God: An Ecofeminist Theology of Earth Healing* (San Francisco: HarperCollins, 1992), esp. chap. 9.

25. Dorothy McDougall, *The Cosmos as Primary Sacrament: The Horizon for an Ecological Sacramental Theology* (New York: Peter Lang, 2003). See also Susan A. Ross, "The Aesthetic and the Sacramental," *Worship* 59 (1985): 2–17.

26. Sallie McFague, *Super, Natural Christians: How We Should Love Nature* (Minneapolis: Fortress Press, 1997), 1.

✓

world as full of subjects, employing Martin Buber's understanding of the I-Thou relationship. Thus in her book the primary model or metaphor for nature is that of subject. To support this model McFague draws on a catholic sacramental tradition. She credits a sacramental worldview for the insight that the world is a symbol of the divine (who is immanent and transcendent) and can help us reach God, an insight that is linked to incarnationalism and an understanding of the intrinsic worth of the world and that encourages the subject model she advocates.[27]

The idea of natural beauty as a kind of training ground for moral pilgrims is an ancient one that carries through much of the history of theological reflection on natural beauty, as explored in chapter one. It is espoused as a source of religious insight by Josiah Royce as well. So the idea that there is a religious dimension to the aesthetic experience of natural beauty is not new. Adding sacramental experience to this process allows for a deeper understanding of the truth that achieving insight from natural beauty, or achieving a sense of beauty, requires cultivation and a spiritual journey. As moral pilgrims, we are also trained by the ongoing life of the sacraments.[28] It is in the very intersection of the aesthetic, the religious, and the sacramental that we are able to see Royce's three marks of insight: breadth of range, coherence and unity of view, and closeness of personal touch.

Love and Passion

If theological aesthetics in general is about what moves the human heart, as García-Rivera has suggested, what, then, is the role of love and passion? Thomas Aquinas wrote that the beautiful is that which,

---

27. Ibid., 26–27.
28. See, for example, Leonel Mitchell, *Praying Shapes Believing: A Theological Commentary on the Book of Common Prayer* (New York: Morehouse, 1991).

when grasped, pleases. Why is it that we are attracted to beautiful places and crave such pleasurable experiences? What can we learn about ourselves from that craving?

In *Super, Natural Christians*, McFague explores a source for the relational model: an aesthetic relation to nature as subject. She draws on Simone Weil and Iris Murdoch to talk about breaking deeply ingrained, flawed, and anti-body/nature habits of attention in favor of trying to see the world as it really is, since, according to Murdoch, "we cannot love that which we do not know" and, as Weil wrote, "absolute attention is prayer." McFague suggests that love and knowledge go hand in hand.[29] The "unutterable particularity of each creature, event, aspect of nature calls forth wonder and delight," and in order to see this particularity, which will inspire an eco-friendly ethics of care, one needs to cultivate what McFague calls the loving eye. Here she borrows the idea of loving vs. arrogant eyes from feminist theorist Marilyn Frye, who writes that there is no such thing as an innocent eye with a view from nowhere. The arrogant eye sees everything in relation to itself, denies complexity and mystery in favor of control and simplicity, and regards women and nature as objects. By contrast, the loving eye acknowledges complexity, mystery, and difference, and respects the other as subject.[30] McFague wants to extend the loving eye in an unsentimental way to the natural world, which would offer a perceptual shift with enormous implications.

A theologian deals with the question of what is real, and Murdoch suggests that love "is the extremely difficult realization that something other than oneself is real. Love . . . is the discovery of reality."[31] McFague and Murdoch seem to share a similar Platonic understanding of the process by which a human viewer is

29. McFague, *Super, Natural Christians*, 29–31.
30. Ibid., 32–34.

"decentered" in the encounter with a subject of nature. In the now famous example of her encounter with a kestrel, Murdoch writes: "I am looking out of my window in an anxious and resentful state of mind, oblivious to my surroundings, brooding perhaps on some damage done to my prestige. Then suddenly I observe a hovering kestrel. In a moment everything is altered. The brooding self with its hurt vanity has disappeared. There is nothing now but kestrel."[32] This process of decentering the ego so that the other can be truly seen and known is essential to religious insight, and it is rooted in love.

Aesthetic interest is about absorption into the particular; the "aesthetic rivets our attention on the other, but in a way that connects us to the other."[33] In terms of theological method, then, seeing nature through the model of subject requires cultivation of the loving eye, the result of which in some sense is a truer and more cherished picture of reality, and thus of God.[34]

And what of desire, passion, and delight in the experience of natural beauty? This seems to be something that is held in common, as evidenced, for example, in the story of the retreat goers at the beginning of this chapter. It is helpful here to consider the ancient idea of the *capax Dei*, found in the works of Augustine and many others, loosely translated as the human capacity to know God. If the experience of the beautiful has a revelatory aspect, perhaps the desire or passion for such experiences is a fundamental quality of the human person. Perhaps it is delight, or what pleases, in the experience of

31. Ibid., 34. See Iris Murdoch, "The Sovereignty of Good Over Other Concepts," 363–85 in eadem, *Existentialists and Mystics: Writings on Philosophy and Literature*, ed. Peter J. Conradi (New York: Penguin Books, 1997), at 369.
32. Ibid.
33. McFague, *Super, Natural Christians*, 136.
34. Carolyn Merchant's work on a partnership ethic achieves the same goal, but without any hint of the romanticism or sentimentality that are presumed to linger in McFague's text. See, for example, Stephen Webb, "Should We All Love Nature? A Critique of Sallie McFague's *Super, Natural Christians*," *Encounter* 59 (1998): 409–19.

natural beauty that draws us beyond ourselves into an ascent toward God as Beauty. Such delight not only feeds our souls, but it can help us to develop the loving eye and be in right relationship with nature. This has the power to move the human heart in much more profound ways than stewardship arguments based on virtue or asceticism.[35]

Transience and Loss

A theological aesthetics studies beauty but does not romanticize it. A cultivation of the sense of beauty would not be complete without an acknowledgment of transience and loss. Augustine knew this, as he saw vestiges of the Trinity in the landscape but knew his spiritual senses were limited by his human, fallen state. Royce knew it, especially as the first World War broke out, as he experienced the illness and death of his loved ones, as his idealism was tempered, and as he endearingly held up lost causes as noble. Goldsworthy embraces transience as part of the natural order of things, letting his work return to its natural state. This is common territory in aesthetics.

I recall a conversation with Alejandro García-Rivera in which he said that a Christian aesthetics will always have an element of theodicy within it. It stems from the crucifixion and resurrection of Christ. He suggested that we look at a crucifix and see beauty, the beauty of the resurrection, but in the midst of death and human sin. It reminds me of Calvin's quickening moment, that sense of conviction of sin even in the midst of beauty, glory, and conversion. It reminds me of Royce's view that a religious insight comes to us from outside sources, including beauty, and serves as a reminder of our need for

---

35. For example, Sallie McFague's *Life Abundant: Rethinking Theology and Economy for a Planet in Peril* (Minneapolis: Fortress Press, 2001), esp. 205–10, "Appendix: A Manifesto to North American Middle-Class Christians." Here she argues for less consumerism and a reconceptualization of abundant life so that more may share in that abundance. It is a powerful argument, but are we too selfish to live by it?

ᵐn. It echoes Royce's understanding of the religious mission of

ᵢ.

A theological aesthetics of nature seeks to understand the experience of natural beauty as redemptive. This includes an honest look at human sin in relation to the environment, and perhaps a certain wistfulness as earthly beauty is destroyed. Thus transience and loss are key to an honest cultivation of the sense of beauty.

Conclusion

I have sought in this chapter to expand the work of the previous three. I have explored additional key elements of a theological aesthetics of nature from different angles, as if spinning a diamond around and exploring its facets. In all of this the guiding questions have been (1) why we crave the experience of natural beauty, and (2) what happens in that experience theologically.

Any current theological reflection on the experience of natural beauty is informed by a long history of such reflection that has origins in ancient Greece. In that history, natural beauty has played many roles in Christian life, even when developments in philosophical aesthetics made it increasingly difficult to consider beauty as somehow divine or transcendent.

Closer to the present day, the nineteenth century brought several important developments in the ways we view nature itself. As Simon Schama has suggested, we cannot view the natural world apart from cultural narratives, and the blessing of this awareness is that we do not need to remain bound by those narratives. This is why the nineteenth-century developments in ways of viewing nature are so critical to a theological aesthetics of nature. Understanding that our use of resources and our need for beauty have the same Puritan roots can help us to rethink our relationship with the natural world in the

American context. A theological aesthetics of nature today, which seeks an understanding of a religious dimension in the experience of natural beauty, is a continuation of the theme of the cross in the wilderness.

A tracing of this history makes clear to us the need for a theory of interpretation of aesthetic experience; one such is provided by Josiah Royce. In developing his hidden aesthetics we can see that natural beauty is a source of religious insight into the need and way of salvation. Such experience draws us redemptively into community, into his Beloved Community now understood as an ecological beloved community dedicated to the cause of ecological redemption. Rooted in ecological theology, this is an interpretation of what Alejandro García-Rivera called the community of the beautiful.

García-Rivera insisted that theological aesthetics, as an emerging field and ground for constructive theology, requires the cultivation of a sense of beauty, a sense that was self-evident before the decline of beauty but that now has largely been lost. To help us cultivate this sense of beauty we turn to the artist (particularly a land artist like Andy Goldsworthy), who offers an experience of the beautiful that can be shared and questions fundamental dualisms in how we understand humanity in relation to nature. The artist also helps us to conceptualize the connection between human and divine creativity. By helping us to truly see natural beauty with a loving eye, the artist taps into a revelatory aspect of natural beauty as that which we both crave and destroy.

The cultivation of a sense of beauty comes through aesthetic, religious, and sacramental experience. Achieving a sense of beauty requires cultivation and a spiritual journey nourished in the ongoing practice of sacramental life. When all three types of experience intersect we are able to see what Royce called the three marks of religious insight: breadth of range, unity of view, and closeness of personal touch.

A theological aesthetics of nature must have a place for love and passion. A desire for natural beauty is part of the human creature, and the experience of beauty is not a neutral, dispassionate endeavor. We crave beauty; we are moved by beauty, and the experience of beauty, the fulfillment of desire, brings us closer to the divine and closer to a right relationship with a created order designed to delight.

Finally, the cultivation of a sense of beauty acknowledges transience and loss in the pilgrim's journey. We cannot truly know earthly beauty without seeing decay. We cannot fully love nature without feeling convicted by its destruction. This is a message as old as Christian faith. There is no grace without sin; there is no life without death. Such is the experience of beauty in a fallen world.

Taken all together, these facets offer a theological aesthetics of nature. The central premise is that the experience of natural beauty is a source of religious insight into the need and the way of salvation. It offers a view of redeemed life as participation in the ecological beloved community of the beautiful. And it offers a view of redeemed life that includes both the human and the natural world.

Conclusion: Saving Beauty

I am writing this on a warm day in early fall, on a quiet street in Little Rock, Arkansas. I look out my window to see the afternoon sun streaming through the trees and casting shadows on the grass. It is a lovely view. It is hard to reconcile the peacefulness of this moment with the complexity of the environmental crisis and all of the politics and economics entangled therein. But as I look out the window I reflect on what a joy it has been to spend time writing about beauty. And I wonder: what if beauty really could save the world? A far-fetched idea to be sure.

And yet, I think about the beauty God created in this world and about how we, as God's creatures, crave that beauty. And I think about how the experience of beauty is revelatory: teaching us something from outside ourselves. Experiencing beauty meets a deep desire within us; it must have been meant to be so. It is part of what makes us human.

Yet it is something that we destroy in our humanness, in our sinful appetites and neglect. That destruction has inspired a vast sea of theological responses and urgent cries for action. Great work has been done on stewardship and asceticism, attempts to answer what is, at its heart, a spiritual crisis.

That urgency gave rise to many parish green teams, one in my own congregation, who gathered to figure out what to do, as the church, about the environmental crisis. We have changed light bulbs, carpooled, housed community-supported agriculture, offered adult and children's formation on the topic, looked at plans for solar panels, and installed a rain barrel in the memorial garden. But as one parishioner so eloquently asked recently, "Now what?" And in her question I could hear fear and despair, that our efforts will not make much of an impact in the bigger scheme of things.

I do not have an answer, but I linger on beauty. I am advocating for beauty out of an intuition that fear and despair will bring us only so far toward ecological well-being. Joy and delight in beauty have the power to move our hearts in a different way, in a way in which our hearts were created to be moved. Our capacity for beauty might be our strongest ally in environmental work.

In this book I have written about human and ecological redemption as two realities already and not yet connected. The catechism of my Episcopal tradition defines redemption as "the act of God which sets us free from the power of evil, sin, and death."[1] A theological aesthetics of nature insists that God, as Beauty, can act to free us from the power of evil, sin, and death in environmental degradation, and that such liberation comes out of the experience of natural beauty.

I look again through the window and watch the sunlight. I give thanks to God for creating something so lovely. And I give thanks for the insight that there might be a sacramental power at work in this moment, offering a new breadth of range, a unity of view, and the closeness of personal touch.

1. *The Book of Common Prayer* (New York: Church Publishing, 1979), 849.

Bibliography

Abram, David. *The Spell of the Sensuous: Perception and Language in a More-than-Human World*. New York: Pantheon Books, 1996.

Aland, Barbara, et al. *The Greek New Testament*. 4th revised ed. Stuttgart: Deutsche Bibelgesellschaft, 2001.

Aristotle. *The Nicomachean Ethics*. Translated by Christopher Rowe. Oxford and New York: Oxford University Press, 2002.

Auquiere, Charles. *La nature photographique d'Andy Goldsworthy*. Bruxelles: La Lettre volée, 2001.

Augustine, Saint. *De musica*. Translated by R. Catesby Taliaferro. In *The Fathers of the Church*, vol. 4. Washington, DC: Catholic University of America Press, 1947.

———. *The Confessions*. Translated by R. S. Pine-Coffin. Harmondsworth: Penguin, 1961.

———. *The Trinity*. Translated by Stephen McKenna. Boston: St. Paul Editions, 1965.

———. *The City of God*. Translated by Henry Bettenson. Harmondsworth: Penguin, 1972.

Ball, Ian, et al., eds. *The Earth Beneath: A Critical Guide to Green Theology*. London: SPCK, 1992.

Balthasar, Hans Urs von. *The Glory of the Lord: A Theological Aesthetics. I: Seeing the Form*. Edited by Joseph Fessio and John Riches. Translated by Erasmo Leiva-Merikakis. New York: Crossroad, 1983.

———. *The Glory of the Lord: A Theological Aesthetics. II: Studies in Theological Style: Clerical Styles*. Edited by John Riches. Translated by Andrew Louth et al. New York: Crossroad, 1984.

Barrett, Clifford, ed. *Contemporary Idealism in America*. New York: The Macmillan Company, 1932.

Baumgarten, Alexander Gottlieb. *Reflections on poetry; Alexander Gottlieb Baumgarten's Meditationes philosophicae de nonnullis ad poema pertinentibus* (1735). Translated by Karl Aschenbrenner and William B. Holther. Berkeley: University of California Press, 1954.

Belting, Hans. *Likeness and Presence: A History of the Image before the Era of Art*, trans. Edmund Jephcott. Chicago: University of Chicago Press, 1994.

Berry, Thomas. *The Great Work: Our Way into the Future*. New York: Bell Tower, 1999.

Besançon, Alain. *The Forbidden Image: An Intellectual History of Iconoclasm*. Translated by Jane Marie Todd. Chicago: University of Chicago Press, 2000.

Beyst, Stefan. "Andy Goldsworthy: The Beauty of Creation." At en.wikipedia.org/wiki/Andy_Goldsworthy. Accessed 24 June 2007.

Boenig, Robert. "Music and Mysticism in Hildegard's *O ignis spiritus paraclit*." *Studia Mystica* 9, no. 3 (Fall 1986): 60–72.

Boff, Leonardo. *Ecology and Liberation: A New Paradigm*. Maryknoll, NY: Orbis Books, 1995.

Bonaventure. *The Mind's Road to God*. Translated by Philotheus Boehner. Indianapolis: Hackett, 1956.

Brown, Frank Burch. *Good Taste, Bad Taste, and Christian Taste: Aesthetics in Religious Life*. New York: Oxford University Press, 2000.

Calvin, Jean. *The Institutes of Christian Religion.* Translated by Ford Lewis Battles. Library of Christian Classics 20. Philadelphia: Westminster Press, 1960.

Carson, Rachel. *Silent Spring.* 40th anniversary ed. Boston: Mariner Books, 2002.

Clendenning, John. *The Life and Thought of Josiah Royce.* Madison, WI: University of Wisconsin Press, 1985.

———, ed. *The Letters of Josiah Royce.* Chicago: University of Chicago Press, 1970.

Cobb, John B. *Is It Too Late? A Theology of Ecology.* Denton, TX: Environmental Ethics Books, 1995.

Debs, Eugene V. *Debs: His Life, Writings and Speeches.* San Francisco: University Press of the Pacific, 2002.

Dillard, Annie. *Holy the Firm.* New York: Perennial, 1977.

Dillenberger, Jane Daggett. *The Religious Art of Andy Warhol.* New York: Continuum, 1998.

Donovan, Molly, and Tina Fiske, eds. *The Andy Goldsworthy Project.* Washington, DC: National Gallery of Art; Thames & Hudson, 2010.

Dupré, Louis. "Hans Urs von Balthasar's Theology of Aesthetic Form." *Theological Studies* 49 (1988): 299–318.

Eco, Umberto. *Art and Beauty in the Middle Ages.* Translated by Hugh Bredin. New Haven: Yale University Press, 1986.

Edwards, Jonathan. *The Works of Jonathan Edwards.* New Haven: Yale University Press, 1980.

———. *The Religious Affections.* Edinburgh: Banner of Truth Trust, 1986.

Emerson, Ralph Waldo. *The Oxford Authors: Ralph Waldo Emerson.* Edited by Richard Poirier. Oxford: Oxford University Press, 1990.

Evans, G. R. *Augustine on Evil.* Cambridge: Cambridge University Press, 1982.

Farley, Edward. *Faith and Beauty: A Theological Aesthetic*. Burlington, VT: Ashgate, 2001.

Focillon, Henri. *The Life of Forms in Art*. New York: Wittenborn, Schultz, 1948.

Fox, Matthew. *Illuminations of Hildegard of Bingen.* Santa Fe, NM: Bear & Co., 1985.

García-Rivera, Alejandro. *The Community of the Beautiful: A Theological Aesthetics*. Collegeville, MN: Liturgical Press, 1999.

———. "The Sense of Beauty and the Talk of God." Graduate Theological Union Distinguished Faculty Lecture, November 13, 2002.

Gebara, Ivone. *Longing for Running Water: Ecofeminism and Liberation*. Translated by David Molineaux. Minneapolis: Fortress Press, 1999.

———. "Yearning for Beauty." *The Other Side* (July–August 2003): 24–25.

Gelpi, Donald. *Varieties of Transcendental Experience: A Study in Constructive Postmodernism*. Collegeville, MN: Liturgical Press, 2000.

Gerbi, Antonello. *Nature in the New World: From Christopher Columbus to Gonzalo Fernandez de Oviedo*. Translated by Jeremy Moyle. Pittsburgh: University of Pittsburgh Press, 1985.

Glacken, Clarence J. *Traces on the Rhodian Shore: Nature and Culture in Western Thought from Ancient Times to the End of the Eighteenth Century*. Berkeley: University of California Press, 1967.

Goldsworthy, Andy. *Andy Goldsworthy: A Collaboration with Nature*. New York: Abrams, 1990.

———. *Andy Goldsworthy: Ice and Snow Drawings, 1990–1992*. Edinburgh: Fruitmarket Gallery, 1992.

———. *Stone*. New York: H. N. Abrams, 1994.

———. "Touchstones." *Circa* 74 (Winter 1995): 43–47.

———. *Andy Goldsworthy: Sheepfolds*. Introduction by Steve Chettle. London: M. Hue-Williams Fine Art, 1996.

———. *Wood: Andy Goldsworthy*. New York: H. N. Abrams, 1996.

———. *Arch.* New York: H. N. Abrams, 1999.

———. *Wall at Storm King: Andy Goldsworthy.* New York: H. N. Abrams, 2000.

———. "Andy Goldsworthy's Stone River." *Cantor Arts Center Journal* 2 (2000–2001): 64–77.

———. *Midsummer Snowballs: Andy Goldsworthy.* London: Thames & Hudson, 2001.

———. *Le temps.* Arcueil: Anthèse, 2001.

———. *Passage: Andy Goldsworthy.* Arceuil: Anthèse, 2004.

Grout, Catherine. "Une esthétique pragmatique." *Art Press* 192 (June 1994): 30–35.

Hegel, G. W. F. *On Art, Religion, and Philosophy: Introductory Lectures to the Realm of Absolute Spirit.* Edited with an introduction by J. Glenn Gray. New York: Harper & Row, 1970.

Hessel, Dieter T. "Christianity and Ecology: Wholeness, Respect, Justice, Sustainability." *Earth Ethics* 10, no. 1 (Fall 1998): 8–10.

———, and Rosemary Radford Ruether, eds. *Christianity and Ecology: Seeking the Well-Being of Earth and Humans.* Cambridge, MA: Harvard University Center for the Study of World Religions, distributed by Harvard University Press, 2000.

Hildegard of Bingen. *Scivias.* Translated by Bruce Hozeski. Santa Fe, NM: Bear & Company, 1986.

Hipple, Walter John. *The Beautiful, the Sublime & the Picturesque in Eighteenth Century British Aesthetic Theory.* Carbondale, IL: Southern Illinois University Press, 1957.

Hofstadter, Albert. *Philosophies of Art and Beauty: Selected Readings in Aesthetics from Plato to Heidegger.* Chicago: University of Chicago Press, 1964.

Hut, Hans. "The Gospel of All Creatures," 64–80 in *Early Anabaptist Spirituality: Selected Writings*. Edited by Daniel Liechty. Classics of Western Spirituality. Mahwah, NJ: Paulist Press, 1994.

Jensen, Robin Margaret. *Understanding Early Christian Art*. New York: Routledge, 2000.

Kant, Immanuel. *Critique of Judgment*. Translated by J. H. Bernard. New York: Hafner, 1951.

Keel, Othmar. *The Symbolism of the Biblical World: Ancient Near Eastern Iconography and the Book of Psalms*. New York: Eisenbrauns, 1997.

Kegley, Jacquelyn Ann. *Genuine Individuals and Genuine Communities: A Roycean Public Philosophy*. Nashville, TN: Vanderbilt University Press, 1997.

———. *Josiah Royce in Focus*. Bloomington: Indiana University Press, 2008.

Kornhauser, Elizabeth, intro. *Hudson River School: Masterworks from the Wadsworth Atheneum Museum of Art*. New Haven: Yale University Press, 2003.

Korsmeyer, Carolyn. *Gender and Aesthetics: An Introduction*. New York: Routledge, 2004.

Krause, Bernie. *The Great Animal Orchestra: Finding the Origins of Music in the World's Wild Places*. New York: Hatchette, 2011.

Kubler, George. *The Shape of Time: Remarks on the History of Things*. New Haven: Yale University Press, 1962.

Kuklick, Bruce. *A History of Philosophy in America, 1720–2000*. Oxford and New York: Clarendon Press, 2001.

Leopold, Aldo. *A Sand County Almanac*. New York: Ballantine Books, 1949.

Lowenstein, Oliver. "Natural Time and Human Experience: Andy Goldsworthy's Dialogue with Modernity." *Sculpture* 22, no. 5 (June 2003): 34–39.

Luther, Martin. *Watchwords for the Warfare of Life*. Translated by Elizabeth Rundle Charles. New York: M. W. Dodd, 1869.

Malpas, William. *The Art of Andy Goldsworthy: Complete Works.* Maidstone: Crescent Moon, 2005.

McDaniel, Jay B. *Of God and Pelicans: A Theology of Reverence for Life.* Louisville: Westminster John Knox, 1989.

McDermott, John, ed. *The Basic Writings of Josiah Royce.* Chicago: University of Chicago Press, 1969.

McDougall, Dorothy. *The Cosmos as Primary Sacrament: The Horizon for an Ecological Sacramental Theology.* New York: Peter Lang, 2003.

McFague, Sallie. *Super, Natural Christians: How We Should Love Nature.* Minneapolis: Fortress Press, 1997.

———. "An Ecological Christology: Does Christianity Have It?" 29–46 In Dieter T. Hessel and Rosemary Radford Ruether, eds., *Christianity and Ecology: Seeking the Well-Being of Earth and Humans.* Cambridge, MA: Harvard University Center for the Study of World Religions, distributed by Harvard University Press, 2000.

———. *Life Abundant: Rethinking Theology and Economy for a Planet in Peril.* Minneapolis: Fortress Press, 2001.

McGrath, Alister E., ed. *The Blackwell Encyclopedia of Modern Christian Thought.* Oxford: Blackwell, 1993.

Merchant, Carolyn. *The Death of Nature: Women, Ecology and the Scientific Revolution.* San Francisco: HarperCollins, 1980.

———. *Earthcare: Women and the Environment.* New York: Routledge, 1995.

———. *Reinventing Eden: The Fate of Nature in Western Culture.* New York: Routledge, 2003.

Metrick, Lenore. "Disjunctions in Nature and Culture: Andy Goldsworthy." *Sculpture* 22, no. 5 (June 2003): 28–33.

Miles, Margaret R. "Vision: The Eye of the Body and the Eye of the Mind in Saint Augustine's *De trinitate* and *Confessions*," *Journal of Religion* 63, no. 2 (April 1983): 125–42.

———. *Image as Insight: Visual Understanding in Western Christianity and Secular Culture.* Boston: Beacon Press, 1985.

———. *Desire and Delight: A New Reading of Augustine's* Confessions. New York: Crossroad, 1991.

———. "Intentions and Effects: Beauty, Pluralism, and Responsibility." *Sewanee Theological Review* 41 (1997): 48–58.

———. "Who is 'We': Augustine's Debate with the Manicheans." *Sewanee Theological Review* 41 (1997): 34–47.

———. *Plotinus on Body and Beauty: Society, Philosophy, and Religion in Third-Century Rome.* Oxford: Blackwell, 1999.

———. Review of *The Community of the Beautiful,* by Alejandro García-Rivera. *Journal of the American Academy of Religion* 68 (2000): 412–13.

———. *The Word Made Flesh: A History of Christian Thought.* Oxford: Blackwell, 2005.

Mitchell, Leonel. *Praying Shapes Believing: A Theological Commentary on the Book of Common Prayer.* New York: Morehouse, 1991.

Moore, Kathleen Dean. "Field Notes for an Aesthetic of Storms," 53–63 in Moore, *Holdfast: At Home in the Natural World.* New York: Lyons Press, 1999.

Motavalli, Jim. "Stewards of the Earth: The Growing Religious Mission to Protect the Environment." *E: The Environmental Magazine* 13, no. 6 (November/December 2002): 2–16.

Murdoch, Iris. "The Sovereignty of the Good," 363–85 in Murdoch, *Existentialists and Mystics: Writings on Philosophy and Literature.* Edited by Peter J. Conradi. New York: Penguin Books, 1997.

Newman, Barbara, ed. *Voice of the Living Light: Hildegard of Bingen and Her World.* Berkeley: University of California Press, 1998.

Niebuhr, Richard R. "Edwards' Idea of Excellency or Beauty." Unpublished class handout, Harvard Divinity School, September 1997.

Oelschlaeger, Max. *The Idea of Wilderness: From Prehistory to the Age of Ecology*. New Haven: Yale University Press, 1991.

Oppenheim, Frank. *Royce's Mature Philosophy of Religion*. Notre Dame, IN: University of Notre Dame Press, 1987.

———. *Royce's Mature Ethics*. Notre Dame, IN: University of Notre Dame Press, 1993.

———. *Reverence for the Relations of Life: Re-imaging Pragmatism via Josiah Royce's Interactions with Peirce, James, and Dewey*. Notre Dame, IN: University of Notre Dame Press, 2005.

———. ed. *Josiah Royce's Late Writings: A Collection of Unpublished and Scattered Works*. 2 vols. Bristol: Thoemmes Press, 2001.

Parker, Kelly A. "Josiah Royce." In *The Stanford Encyclopedia of Philosophy (Continually Updated Resource: Summer 2005 Edition)*. Edited by Edward N. Zalta. URL http://plato.stanford.edu/archives/sum2005/entries/royce/, accessed 11/12/12.

Peirce, Charles Sanders. *The Essential Peirce: Selected Philosophical Writings*. Volumes 1 and 2. Edited by Nathan Houser, et al. Bloomington: Indiana University Press, 1998.

Plato. *Greater Hippias*. Translated by H. N. Fowler. Loeb Classical Library, Plato IV. Cambridge, MA: Harvard University Press, 1977.

———. *Timaeus*. Translated by Donald Zeyl. Indianapolis: Hackett, 2000.

Plotinus. *The Enneads. Plotinus, English and Greek with an English translation by A. H. Armstrong*. 7 vols. Cambridge, MA: Harvard University Press, 1966–1988.

Plumwood, Val. *Feminism and the Mastery of Nature*. New York: Routledge, 1993.

———. *Environmental Culture: The Ecological Crisis of Reason*. New York: Routledge, 2002.

Proudfoot, Wayne. *Religious Experience*. Berkeley: University of California Press, 1985.

Pseudo-Dionysius. *The Divine Names; and Mystical Theology.* Translated by John D. Jones. Milwaukee: Marquette University Press, 1980.

Rahner, Karl. "La doctrine des 'Sens Spirituels' au Moyen-Age," *Revue d'Ascétique et de Mystique* 14, no. 55 (1933): 263–99.

Reese, Thomas F. "Andy Goldsworthy's New Ruins" 25–34 in *Mortality Immortality? The Legacy of 20th-Century Art.* Los Angeles: Getty Conservation Institute, 1998.

Regimbald, Manon. *D'entre les arts, l'in situ. Mosaic* 31, no. 4 (December 1998): 99–121.

Riedelsheimer, Thomas. *Rivers and Tides: Andy Goldsworthy Working with Time* [videorecording]. Mediopolis Film with Skyline Productions, Ltd., 2004.

Ross, Susan. "The Aesthetic and the Sacramental." *Worship* 59 (1985): 2–17.

Royce, Josiah. *Studies in Good and Evil: A Series of Essays upon Problems of Philosophy and Life* [1898]. New York: D. Appleton and Company, 1906.

———. *The Philosophy of Loyalty.* New York: Macmillan, 1908.

———. *The World and the Individual.* 2 vols [1899–1901]. New York: Macmillan, 1908.

———. *The Sources of Religious Insight* [1912]. Washington, DC: Catholic University of America Press, 2001.

———. *The Problem of Christianity* [1913]. Washington, DC: Catholic University of America Press, 2001.

———. *The Hope of the Great Community.* New York: Macmillan, 1916.

———. "Mind," "Monotheism," "Negation," and "Order," in vol. 8 of *Encyclopaedia of Religion and Ethics.* Edited by James Hastings. New York: Charles Scribner's Sons, 1916.

Ruether, Rosemary Radford. *Gaia & God: An Ecofeminist Theology of Earth Healing.* San Francisco: HarperCollins, 1989.

———, ed. *Women Healing Earth: Third World Women on Ecology, Feminism, and Religion.* Maryknoll, NY: Orbis Books, 1996.

Sagan, Carl, et al. "An Open Letter to the Religious Community." January, 1990. URL http://earthrenewal.org/Open_letter_to_the_religious_.htm.

Sampson, Paula K. "Deep Christianity: Land, Liturgy and Environmental Virtue Ethics in Northwestern British Columbia." Ph.D. diss., Graduate Theological Union, 1999.

Schama, Simon. *Landscape and Memory*. New York: Knopf, 1995.

———. "The Stone Gardener: A Land Artist Comes to Lower Manhattan." *The New Yorker* 79, no. 27 (September 22, 2003): 126–32.

Scarry, Elaine. *On Beauty and Being Just*. Princeton, NJ: Princeton University Press, 1999.

Schaefer, Jamie. "Appreciating the Beauty of Earth." *Theological Studies* 62 (March 2001): 23–52.

Scharper, Stephen B. *Redeeming the Time: A Political Theology of the Environment*. New York: Continuum, 1997.

Smith, John E. *Royce's Social Infinite: The Community of Interpretation*. NY: Liberal Arts, 1950.

———. *Experience and God.* New York: Fordham University Press, 1995.

———, ed. *A Jonathan Edwards Reader*. New Haven: Yale University Press, 1995.

Southgate, Christopher. *The Groaning of Creation: God, Evolution, and the Problem of Evil*. Louisville: Westminster John Knox, 2008.

Stoll, Mark. *Protestantism, Capitalism, and Nature in America*. Albuquerque: University of New Mexico Press, 1997.

Tartarkiewicz, Wladyslaw. "The Great Theory of Beauty and Its Decline." *Journal of Aesthetics and Art Criticism* 31 (1972): 165–79.

———. *A History of Ideas: An Essay in Aesthetics*. Warsaw: Polish Scientific Publishers, 1980.

Thomas Aquinas, Saint. *De Veritate*. 3 vols. Translated by Robert W. Mulligan. Chicago: Regnery, 1952–1954 (qq. 1, 2, 10, 22, 26).

———. *Summa Theologiae.* Cambridge: Blackfriars; New York: McGraw-Hill, 1964–1981. (*Pars Prima,* qq. 5, 12, 35-39, 67, 84-86, 91; *Prima Secundae,* qq. 21, 27, 49, 57, 77; *Secunda Secondae,* qq. 96, 141, 145, 168, 180; *Supplementum,* q. 83).

Thomas, Owen C. *Theological Questions: Analysis and Argument.* Wilton, CT: Morehouse-Barlow, 1983.

———. *What Is It That Theologians Do, How They Do It, and Why: Anglican Essays.* Lewiston: Edwin Mellen, 2006.

Tucker, Mary Evelyn. "Worldly Wonder: Religions Enter an Ecological Phase." *E: The Environmental Magazine* 13, no. 6 (November/December 2002): 12–14.

Webb, Stephen. "Should We All Love Nature? A Critique of Sallie McFague's *Super, Natural Christians.*" *Encounter* 59 (1998): 409–19.

Wendell, François. *Calvin: The Origins and Development of His Religious Thought,* trans. Philip Mairet. New York: Harper & Row, 1963.

White, Lyn. "The Historical Roots of Our Ecologic Crisis." *Science,* n. s. 155, no. 3767 (1967): 1203–07.

Wolterstorff, Nicholas. *Art in Action: Toward a Christian Aesthetic.* Grand Rapids: Eerdmans, 1980.

Wood, Christopher S. *Albrecht Altdorfer and the Origins of Landscape.* Chicago: University of Chicago Press, 1993.

Index

CPSIA information can be obtained at www.ICGtesting.com
Printed in the USA
LVOW01s1014090714

393530LV00004B/4/P